D0128021

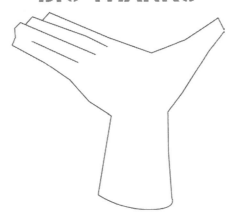

This book would not be possible without the following people who believed in us from the beginning, who worked with us when we had a kernel of an idea, and who saw us through to the end:

A Special thanks to Hornbill Service Management for generously contributing many of the metrics outlined within, and a big shout-out to Patrick Bolger for his invaluable additions and wisdom now included in Service Desk Manager's Crash Course.

Mark Brady – The copywriting and branding genius behind the design/graphics of the book as well as a few of the edits. You allowed us to get this done on time and on budget. Find him here: alchemysite.com

Every other Service Desk Manager in the world that we've ever met: If you've heard us speak, or spoken to us, you've touched our lives forever. Though we may not remember your name, you matter to us. This book is for you!

And to anyone we might have missed - You rock, and we appreciate you, too!

A Special note: As mentioned above, this book wouldn't be possible without the contributions of many. But it also wouldn't be possible without the existence of a previous collaboration, The Help Desk Manager's Crash Course. For that work, and for his ideas, we'll be forever grateful to Jeffrey Brooks.

FOREWORD

MALCOLM FRY, AUTHOR & ITIL® INNOVATOR

Too often we direct the majority of our training and education to deliver on the job competence and certification but invest very little on preparing our staff, or indeed ourselves, for their future careers. You could argue that the real skill is in preparing staff for their next step so that they can fully realise their potential. The result is that frequently when staff is promoted they do not have the knowledge or experience to perform the tasks required by their new job. When I was promoted to my first managerial role the first task I had to perform was to prepare and give staff appraisals with no training or education whatsoever. I'm sure you can imagine what a traumatic experience that was for everyone.

Two things I learned very early in my managerial career were to; one, train people to meet their potential and two, don't wait for others - educate yourself. This is where this excellent publication enters the story because it has two uses; one for managers to give to their staff to start working on the future and two for individuals to buy it themselves to start self-education. One of my favourite expressions is "experience is something you get just after you needed it." The Service Desk Manager's Crash Course to a large degree makes this expression redundant because the amount of knowledge in the course is vast.

If you looking to become a manager the Service Desk Manager's Crash Course will help you to prepare yourself, if you are already a manager you can use the Service Desk Manager's Crash Course to help you to refresh and improve your skills, if you are a trainer the Service Desk Manager's Crash Course will make a great course workbook and finally if you will be competing with other staff members for a Service Managers job the chances are that the best prepared will get the job.

Malcolm Fry is a world-renowned IT industry luminary, father of the modern ITIL movement, and author of many bestselling books on IT Service Management.

GETTING STARTED WITH SERVICE DESK MANAGER'S CRASH COURSE

Service Desk Manager's Crash Course was developed by someone who loves the Service Desk Industry: Me. After a decade-plus witnessing and participating in the breakneck-speed of changes in the IT and Technology realms, there's no shortage of lessons-learned. I've done my best to relate the best of this experience managing, leading, and working with inspiring service providers and problem solvers and this edition attempts to reveal some of that collected exploration and wisdom with you.

For the new manager, use this book to quickly get yourself and your Service Desk up to speed, with sections on hiring, discipline, and metrics shallow enough to not overwhelm you, but deep enough that you'll be able to use it for years to come.

For the experienced manager, you'll find years of practice and up-to-the-moment trends condensed into book form, offering a practical take on what's gotten the best results over the years.

I hope you enjoy the finished product, and whether you're a new or experienced manager, that you learn something from your investment that pays big dividends professionally.

One final note: If your company has policies that are in complete contradiction to what we recommend, do what your company says, at least for a little while. See if you can work in our suggestions over time, but don't feel like everything we say must be implemented at once.

To your success,

Phil, and friends.

CONTENTS

SERVICE DESK MANAGERS CRASH COURSE

PHIL GERBYSHAK

CHAPTER 1. HIRE THE BEST,

FORGET THE REST

The best advice ever given is to hire people smarter than yourself; hire the best available candidate every time you have an opening.

Long term, this seems so simple; it's the I/O principle at work: good people/ good results; bad people/ bad results or, as programmers know, garbage in/garbage out. However, short term needs often overcome the long-term results you crave.

- Call volume is high;

- Hold times are long;

- Your team is complaining that they are overworked;

- You feel overworked;

- You ARE overworked;

How can you hire the best, forget the rest and shorten the hiring cycle?

1. Know what you are looking for to round out your team.

Your team doesn't need another person with skills identical to the current team, but, similarly, you don't need to hire the entire laundry list, AKA, dream candidate, so **understand the hole(s) you need to fill.**

Is it a technical leader, a report writer, someone ITIL certified, someone who can do-it-all, a trainer, etc? Be specific, realistic and understand exactly what you need or you'll never find it. This includes recognizing both the opportunities you can offer and the limitations you have, such as compensation, growth, etc.

2) Understand your company culture, as well as your department's, your team's (yes, your team has its own culture) and the support culture you project to your clients.

Candidates don't have to be an exact match, but their attitudes need to be synergistic with the team and support cultures at the least. Remember that you want to add mental diversity in order to challenge and improve the support culture and help take your team to the next level.

If you're reading this book, chances are you're not satisfied with the status quo and want to create a better team, a stronger team. Improving the team isn't about hiring someone to stir the pot, it's about hiring someone who fits in yet still challenges folks to improve.

QUALITIES AND ABILITIES

The best support professionals share many of the same qualities. Rate each of these qualities on a scale of 1-5, with 1 being low and 5 being high. Start things off by rating yourself and your existing team; this will help you to understand where the holes are, so you can achieve the most productive hire.

Attitude is a non-negotiable.

This isn't a case of looking for Pollyannas, or folks with blind optimism that can't see when things are wrong, or "people like me" to build your team; what you want are folks who will look for the possibility in the problem; that see the glass as half-full and look for ways to fix things instead of just complaining that they suck.

How do you find out if someone has a great attitude?

Ask a few questions about difficult times in their career, or when they've dealt with a difficult customer. Listen to the words used. Negative words equal a negative person. Positive words equal a positive person.

Listen for words such as:

- Whiner;
- Annoying;
- Complaining;
- Any other words that focus on the person instead of the situation.

And positive words such as

- Challenge;
- Opportunity;
- We worked together;
- Our team; and
- Additional words that focus on solutions instead of problems.

Communication skills are non-negotiable.

Support center professionals must be great communicators, with especially strong inter-personal communication skills.

Both written and verbal communications are important skills, but it is the requirements of **your** support center that determine which is most important. Once you decide you should hire accordingly.

How can you find someone with great verbal communication skills?

Ask them to describe something with step-by-step instructions. One of my favorite questions is this: *"Walk me through making a peanut butter and jelly sandwich, assuming I know nothing about peanut butter and jelly sandwiches."*

Stay aware of the conversational flow during the interview; arrange multiple interviews with people in different parts of the company, including **at least one person at a lower (admin) level (often the most telling interview)**. Request feedback to assess the candidate's comfort level, verbal skills, respect, etc.

How do you find someone with great written communication skills?

- Review their resume. Are sentences complete and jargon free? Ask someone who isn't in IT to review it; can she understand it, the type of position for which the candidate is applying and what he's doing currently.

- Ask for a sample of documentation she's written in the past or have her write up how-to instructions for a problem common to your support desk. It needs to be easily understood, but not necessarily, the same as you or your team explain it.

- If she sends a thank you note is it specific to your conversation, does it address any questions raised during the interview? Does it indicate real enthusiasm for the job, i.e., does she ask for it? Or was it a generic *"Thanks for interviewing me,"* that leaves you wondering if she downloaded a template.

SKILLS AND EXPERIENCE

(Example only, you need to customize this for your own requirements)

1) Inbound call center/service desk experience is standard, but you should evaluate *where* they got the experience. If the center has a reputation for poor or spotty service, you need to dig to find your candidate's attitude, as opposed to the old manager's.

2) Expertise in whatever technologies are used and at whatever level is required, for example: Microsoft Office 2010, specifically Outlook, Word and Excel; some understanding of incident/problem/call tracking tools, the ability to use the Help menu in a program and the ability to Google to find other answers.

3) Demonstrated excellence in previous positions; awards such as Associate of the month, Analyst of the Year (if available), glowing reviews, career progression, etc.

4) Technical skills/certifications (HDI Certifications, MCP, MCDST, MCSA, A+, etc.) acquired through work and independently.

5) What is her passion? Passion for one thing can be tapped for another. Questions to ask yourself: Does this candidate have any passion? If so, can your position tap into the passion this candidate exhibits?

CHAPTER 2. MARKETING YOUR SERVICE DESK: FROM HELPLESS TO HELPFUL

One of the major ways to thrive as an IT manager is to market your team to the rest of the company as a group of professionals who excel at what they do **and want to help**.

As a manager, marketing your team is serious business and you should do it at every opportunity.

If folks don't know what your team does, you stand a good chance of having your staffing levels cut, of losing the respect of your organization or, worst of all, being considered a commodity instead of an invaluable resource that contributes to the bottom line.

This is true whether you manage in-house support or an out-sourced team; whether it is domestic or offshore.

MOVING FROM HELPLESS TO HELPFUL

1. Get out from behind your desk.

- Make time every week to spend with managers in other areas, not just your department, to find out what they are focusing on, and how your team can add value to the process. This is not a time to share solutions or defend actions, it is a time to be a sponge and listen. **Ask questions, take notes, and learn**.

- If you're not physically close to your peers, do the same thing on the phone. Ask other managers what IT can do to make their lives easier, less stressful, more productive or

  more profitable. Take the opportunity to tune into the other manager's moods, needs, and ways you can improve and provide them even better service in the future—don't offer solutions or defend actions, if someone needs to rant, let them rant. You can learn far more from a rant than from carefully edited dialog.

2. Invite managers from other areas to visit and observe what your team does day-to-day—if folks don't know what you do, then how can they value it?

- Arrange for them to meet your team and observe them at work; if possible allow them to sit in on some calls. Doing this has two benefits...
  - It gives them a greater appreciation for what your team does; and
  - It gives your team a better appreciation for the person on the other end of the phone/email/ other communication channel when they ask for assistance in the future.

3. Get involved outside of your department and find ways to relate it back to your team.

Some possibilities are serving on committees, speaking engagements, writing articles for other departments, helping them set up and use various Web 2.0 efforts, such as wikis, Facebook, blogs, etc.

Marketing your team means working longer hours, but the efforts offer high ROI for both you and your team.

By finding opportunities to network with front-line managers, you learn much more about the customer service they provide and how to include it in your team's offerings.

This kind of interaction gives you a far better understanding of your company's business and that, in turn, gives you more ammunition to show how IT can contribute to the bottom line.

CHAPTER 3. EMPLOYEE ENGAGEMENT:
HELPING YOU KEEP YOUR BEST

Employee engagement has been around for decades, if not centuries; what it's called changes, but the need or the value for it has remained constant.

WHAT IS EMPLOYEE ENGAGEMENT AND WHY IS IT IMPORTANT TO YOU?

Employee engagement: *When given a choice, employees will act in the best interest of their company or their team, instead of working in their own self-interest.*

Gallup's research shows that most workers are not engaged, or worse, they are actively disengaged, from, their work. As a result, managers are struggling to develop engaged teams, and companies are having difficulties fielding engaged workforces.

More actively engaged employees mean less turnover, higher performance, and more satisfied customers and colleagues than less engaged employees do. More engagement equals less time you will spend getting folks to do even the most basic tasks.

Gallup has 12 questions they ask (called the Q12™) that you can use to see if your folks are engaged or disengaged. Some managers recommend against asking people to respond to the survey themselves, preferring to take time to observe team members' behaviors and understand them for themselves.

However, the most valuable information is gained by DOING BOTH and comparing the results, with **the highest value found in the differences between your perceptions and hers.**

GALLUP'S Q12™ POLL

How satisfied are you with your place of employment as a place to work? (Rate on a scale of 1-5)

1. I know what is expected of me at work.

2. I have the materials and equipment I need to do my work right.

3. At work, I have the opportunity to do what I do best every day.

4. In the last seven days, I have received recognition or praise for doing good work.

5. My supervisor, or someone at work, seems to care about me as a person.

6. There is someone at work who encourages my development.

7. At work, my opinions seem to count.

8. The mission or purpose of my organization makes me feel my job is important.

9. My associates or fellow employees are committed to doing quality work.

10. I have a best friend at work.

11. In the last six months, someone at work has talked to me about my progress.

12. This last year, I have had opportunities at work to learn and grow.

The information available on engagement in its various forms would fill multiple hard drives, but for an excellent, ongoing engagement education, we highly recommend David Zinger's *Employee Engagement Network*

(http://employeeengagement.ning.com/).

CHAPTER 4. EFFECTIVE MANAGERS:

DISCIPLINE AND THE RISCC MODEL

Every manager hates dealing with behavioral problems, but that's a big part of what you are paid for. Dealing with them can require anything from a quiet word in private to a complete paper trail ending in termination. Whatever you do, don't minimize the documentation. First, it's of benefit to the employee because it clarifies exactly what the problem is; it's also of benefit to you and your company as due process in the event of a threatened or filed lawsuit. It's not really about discipline, it's about cause and effect—the consequences of actions.

RISCC MODEL

R = Report: When you observe unacceptable behavior evaluate it. Is it an unacceptable act, such as being constantly late back from lunch or does it break company policy, such as some kind of harassment?

I = Impact: Define exactly what effect the specific behavior is having on the team, customers, and other departments.

To do this, YOU need to know what is important to each group and what the full impact was of the offense. It does not have to have a hard impact, such as breaking a law or costing your company millions in lost revenue. Most problem behaviors are softer, such as affecting the team's ability to function effectively or customers experiencing longer than usual hold times.

Employees rarely think about the domino effect of their actions, such as returning a few minutes late from lunch, which affects the entire team's schedule.

S = Specify: This is the part that many managers find the most difficult, discussing it with the offender.

No matter how serious the offense, the key is to focus on the offending behavior, **not on the person.** Focusing on the person turns a behavioral issue into a personal attack and makes solving it far more difficult.

In private, describe and discuss the problem behavior with the offender being sure NOT to apologize for bringing it up. Keep the focus on that person, explaining that the behavior is unacceptable regardless of others doing it. However, if others are doing the same or similar behaviors you need to confirm that and then deal with each one immediately.

For certain types of behavior it can help to find out why it's happening. The person who is chronically late for work may be dealing with a child care issue that you can help solve, eliminating the negative effects, while increasing his loyalty, respect and engagement.

C = Consequences: Many people don't realize that a particular action has consequences (cause and effect); some newer employees have never been held accountable for their actions while growing up, so don't you be surprised if their reaction is surprise and hurt feelings.

Consequences usually don't come into play in the initial discussions (above), but they do on repeat offenses.

If you do get to this point the discussion gets more serious and should be in writing, including

- A description of the behavior;
- How it needs to change;
- What happens if it does not change, including termination if appropriate; and
- A timeline for the changes.

Remember, there's no such thing as a goal without a due date.

The critical factor in consequences is that they

- Fit the impact described above; and are
- Fair;
- Well-defined; and
- Doable.

Consequences should never sound like threats; actions have consequences while threats are against people.

C = Commitment: the final step is the agreement to change the behavior.

Since the initial discussion is informal, agreement about the behavior, correction and timeline may be verbal.

But, if the situation progresses to a written review, agreement requires you to completely explain the behavior, the two of you have discussed it and then **both of you sign it**.

DISCIPLINE PITFALLS:

- Failing to address the situation immediately: If the behavior has a big impact on the team or breaks company policy why did you wait until the seventh time before saying anything? That is unfair to the team, the individual and you.

- Beware of focusing on the individual instead of the behavior.

- Being too broad: The RISCC model works best when you address one specific incident, not as a general "you need improvement in every area" feedback model.

- Piling it on: Also known as dumping, this is the most heinous of all offenses you do as a manager. This completely takes your associates off-guard and leads to you attacking the individual instead of focusing on fixing the specific behavior.

- Failing to prepare for sidebars: You can easily be sidetracked if you're not prepared. Take 15 minutes before the conversation is scheduled and write out each of your points and consider items and distracters the employee may bring up. If you don't, you can and you probably **WILL** be sidetracked.

- Whether informal (verbal) or formal (written), it is necessary for the employee to understand the problem and agree to the solution or nothing will change.

- Never threaten or say something that you are not prepared to do. If you say that X will happen then X needs to happen or you will damage your credibility and make your job as manager far more difficult.

CHAPTER 5. DELEGATING FOR EFFICIENCY

DO YOUR FRIENDS CALL YOUR BLACKBERRY A CRACKBERRY?

- Do you like to tell everyone how your smart phone never stops vibrating, making you a true mobile work warrior?
- Do you tell people that you work until Midnight because it ensures you won't have any surprises in the morning?
- Do you ever say, "If I want it done right, I'll just do it myself!"
- Do you believe that "It will just be faster if I do it myself!"
- Are you busy with work or just doing busy-work?

You already know that you should be delegating, so why aren't you?

There are four main reasons why people don't delegate

1. **Lack of trust** – The day you accepted your promotion to management was the day you bet your future success on your people. That means you have no choice but to trust them, because there is NOTHING you can do hands on that will offset an under or non-performing team. Trust issues often stem from your own insecurity and that means you have a choice to make. Either you can become a slave to your insecurities or you can learn to handle them.
2. **No one can do it as well as me** – This attitude comes over as sheer arrogance, but usually stems from insecurities. (See above.)
3. **Control** – Two issues fall under control. The easy one is a desire to make sure that nothing goes wrong and it stems from trust issues, which we've already mentioned. The second is nastier; it encompasses the desire to control the people to whom you delegate, usually by forcing them to return to you repeatedly to get the information they need to do the work, whether to build up your own ego, for political reasons or to prove how much you're needed.
4. **Job security** – Doing everything is usually an effort to make yourself (seem) indispensible, as is insinuating yourself into every task.

Don't think you can delegate? Ask yourself this key question:

What would happen to your team if you were hit by a truck or were chosen to serve for an extended jury trial? Would it keep functioning or would it fall apart?

THE TRUE KEY TO DELEGATING EFFECTIVELY

When you delegate, you are not only delegating the right to perform an action, you are delegating the right to make the decisions.

If you delegate a task without enough information and authority to accomplish it, you are setting your people and yourself up to fail!

This is the primary rule of delegation; the most important thing for you to understand. If you don't accept this, you will become that most disliked of all managers, the micromanager. Of course, you will get a lot of hiring experience, because of your turnover.

WHEN/WHY SHOULD YOU DELEGATE?

It's not your job to know more than everyone else on your team; as with most things in life, the key is to know where to get the answers.

When delegating, it's mandatory to **think it through first**. Don't make the mistake of casually saying "Hey, Jean, will you do X," and then blaming Jean because you didn't think the delegation through completely. A few considerations when you are ready to delegate:

- **Capability** - Can the person you are considering actually do the required work, since good intentions won't get the job done? Choosing people who lack the necessary skills sets them up to fail, but the black mark will be against YOU for a poor management choice.
- **Commitment** - People get work done that they own; work for which they feel responsible. That is why you must **delegate the information and the authority along with the task**. You can keep final approval, but if they have to keep running to you every two minutes, there will be no ownership.
- **Time to delegate effectively** - This may sound like an oxymoron, but it goes more into the skill of how to actually delegate and selecting the right person, which we will cover in greater detail later in this chapter. You need to make the time to sit down and go over the task as appropriate to the person to whom you will be delegating.

Remember, when you delegate, you are not delegating the right to perform an action; you are delegating the right to make decisions.

WHAT SHOULD BE DELEGATED?

Delegation is all about making you more efficient in what you should be focusing on as the manager of a service desk.

Routine tasks
Routine tasks eat time and can give you a false sense of accomplishment. Additionally, you are taking opportunities away from your team members, since doing things that are routine for you can help someone else grow.

Before delegating routine items, be sure that they are necessary. There are dozens of tasks that stay on a department's to-do list long after they are needed, so **don't delegate what you can eliminate**. Always ask yourself if the activity is needed; what value does it add or need does it fill. If the answer is none, then don't delegate it, eliminate it.

You'll find a list similar to the following one in almost any department, but because the tasks are routine, the list is rarely re-evaluated for current need.

- Fact-finding assignments
- Preparation of rough drafts of reports
- Problem analysis and suggested actions
- Collection of data for reports
- Photocopying, printing, collating
- Data entry

Once you re-evaluate the list, the remaining tasks are easily delegated and have the benefit of being a learning/skill-honing experience for team members.

Complex tasks
Delegating only the menial tasks and keeping the high-level items for you is an act of managerial greed. It isn't that they can't be delegated; rather it's done because these tasks are sexy, high profile and fun—no matter how challenging.

Complex tasks are such things as

- Call and workflow studies
- Data analysis
- Preparation of reports
- Sitting on steering committees
- Being a member of a project or task force
- New software evaluation

The thought process and actions are the same no matter which type of task you are delegating. Remember to give all required information and make sure they know that it's OK to ask questions during the process and be sure that your expectations are in line with the described task. For example, if you ask for a rough draft, without defining "rough" then you can't complain about the result.

If you have **not** been sharing the work, your team members will not know why something is needed or what you want. If you don't tell them you have not right to complain or criticize.
In a perfect world, people at any level would be happy do the tasks assigned, but as you well know, that world is strictly imaginary. Instead, you will have people insist that certain tasks are either…

- Beneath them;
- Above them; or
- Not part of their job description.

The smaller the service desk the more often you'll have resistance, because your team members are already very busy. It's up to you as a manager to be firm about the routine tasks as you are with any other task. Your team will also be more willing when they see you sharing the fun ones, too.

Engagement is best accomplished by taking the time to explain the task's value and why it is important to the team and the company, but if you can't explain why don't expect your team to buy-in.

Once a task is assigned, including delivery date, manage it the same way you would manage any assigned task. Be sure that your people understand that you don't assign busy work and that no matter how small the task it is imperative that it be completed on time and correctly for the benefit of the organization.

Lower level tasks should be assigned, organized and tracked in the same way as any higher–level task

Steps:
1. Explain the importance and the big picture related to the tasks;
2. Assign the tasks fairly;
3. Create a cycle system to ensure tasks are assigned across the board;
4. Work with staff from other departments and train them as necessary; and
5. Track small tasks in the same way you track larger ones.

When delegating always try to assign the project so the person learns something and feels a bit stretched. This doesn't mean that higher-level people aren't assigned lower level tasks; it
means that you find something in the task that will stretch the person to whom it's assigned, even if it's speed.

Explain that additional tasks mean more responsibilities, whether minor or major, and helps prepare them for promotion. But what if, at that time and for a variety of reasons, a team member doesn't want additional responsibilities or to move up? Is it in your or the team's best interest to force it? The short answer is a resounding 'no'! The long answer is more complicated.

Why wouldn't someone want to be promoted? The answer falls into one of two categories.

1. **There are times in a person's life that they just have nothing extra to give.** Therefore, piling on more responsibilities or offering a promotion becomes not only counterproductive, but even destructive. Perhaps a child, parent or someone equally close is critically ill or has died; the employee herself could have been diagnosed with a serious problem; there are many possible reasons and it's your responsibility as their manager to talk privately with them and together determine a course of action. If you have never dealt with a problem of this nature talk to a more senior manager or HR. You need to know what's happening, but you want to be sensitive,

2. **Different people have different capacities.** It's part of your managerial duties to understand that and know when a team member is at their capacity. Preparing someone for a promotion that will take her beyond her capabilities is unfair and has destroyed careers and people. Capacity can be increased over time with exercise, but, like a muscle, it can't go beyond its full growth, although that is often more than people realize.

Finally, when you need to delegate to folks outside of your direct team remember that life is about relationships, and while they are probably interested in expanding their knowledge and enhancing their skills, helping you is quid pro quo. That means that at some point in the future when they need your assistance, you give it graciously.

9 KEYS TO SUCCESSFUL DELEGATION

Overview

- Be aware of the competency and management needs of each of your team or anyone else you ask— you don't want to get them in over their heads.
- Delegate the objective, not the procedure.
- Outline the desired results, not the methodology.
- Be sure to hand off the authority to accomplish the task along with the task.
- Ask people to provide progress reports. Set milestones and interim deadlines to review how things are going.
- Spread delegation around to give people new experiences as part of their training.

Delegation starts with a discussion; that may mean your entire team or a small group if you are looking for a volunteer or one-on-one if you have chosen someone.

There are eight points to cover, write them down and check them off. Doing this gives you more confidence, especially when you first start delegating, and you are sure to cover everything.

1) **Describe the job, in detail and don't hold back information.** Holding back is unfair; it sets people up to fail and makes you a control freak. The description should be interesting and highlight the learning potential.

2) **Make sure the person (your choice or the volunteer) wants to successfully accomplish the task.**

3) **Ask how she plans to tackle the project.** Discuss her plan; help her set milestones and interim deadlines. Again, check to be sure she has all the required information including due date, financial and resource constraints, etc. Coach and mentor her. This is the time to be sure that you have confidence in her means and methods **even if they are different from yours.**

4) **Play Devil's Advocate so the two of you can test the plan.** Consider the pros and cons of various approaches and make sure that you have given complete information. The goal is to eliminate surprises for both you and her.

5) **No matter how well planned stuff happens.** She needs to know that you will be available to help if it is truly necessary. Offer plenty of help during the planning portion, but do NOT micromanage the task. If you do, you are telling her that you do not trust her to do it correctly. If you really believe that then you chose the wrong person.

6) **Double check her willingness to go forward.** This is especially important when you have asked for volunteers in some type of group setting. Often it isn't until someone goes through a task plan that she realizes she may have bit off more than she can chew. It's your responsibility as her manager to analyze if she really is over her head or if it's just a case of cold feet.

7) **Confirm all milestones, interim deadlines for review and the final delivery date.** It may feel like overkill to you, but it is critical to be sure that they are correct and very clearly set in both your minds. Even if there is no hard deadline in fact set a due date. Any task without a real due date will keep being pushed off in favor of those that have one.

8) **The last thing to ask is, "Is there anything else you need to get started?"** At that point, she should tell you anything else she might need beyond what is in the plan—help, resources, time, money, etc.

9.) **Now comes the commitment.** Making the commitment means that you hand-off the task and your person takes it over. Even with all the prep and full confidence you may find this difficult in the beginning (it gets easier with practice), but you need to **let go**. If you don't honestly let go **the person has no reason to take responsibility**. This sets you **both** up to fail.

Having gone through the above process, you are all set to sit back and wait for your team to start achieving the tasks you delegate,

If you believe that, you will also have plenty of time to work on your resume and start searching for a new job.

It isn't a case of not having confidence in your people, but you do need to recognize the fundamental truth that people, even people with the same title and pay grade, are not all the same. It's not rocket science, but managers, especially newer managers, tend to forget this in the press of getting things done.

People not only differ between hiring levels, but they also differ within each level because some need more management, while others need less, but both are valuable to the team.

THE PEOPLE SQUARE

That last statement has a key thought. While micromanaging is always considered a negative different types of people do require different levels of management to perform their best. There is always a give and take. People who require more management are often newer, have less experience or are very laid back, whereas those who are self–starters, highly experienced or with a lot of initiative may need less, although this isn't always a given.

The best teams have a mix of all types in all categories. You might think that it would be better to have all your people with relevant MS degrees and MBAs, but, aside from the cost being impractical, they would still need varying degrees of management.

Obviously, budget is always the first consideration, but what is second?

Growth!

Done well, delegating speeds the professional development of your team, which, in turn, raises their productivity and moral and makes you look good to your boss.

1. Create a simple skills matrix for your team. A skills matrix applies to any industry and is easily done using Excel; below is a generic example and there is a detailed example from an IT desk is available in the Resources section in the back of the book. Be sure to change the skills based on you business, company and the type of assistance your team provides:

    [In order to better reproduce the matrix for copying, see next page.]

Legend
0 = No skill
1 – Beginning
2 – Intermediate
3 – Expert

TECHNICAL

Applicable to your business	Skill 1	Skill 2	Skill 3	Skill 4	Skill 5
Associate					
Associate					

Skill Level Average
(Target 2.3)

PROFESSIONAL SOFT
SKILLS

Applicable to your business	Time Management	Prioritization	Teamwork	Phone	Technical Writing
Associate					
Associate					

Skill Level (Target 2.3)

PERSONAL SOFT
SKILLS

Applicable to your business	Attitude	Initiative	Willingness/ Helpful	Critical Thinking	Trust
Associate					
Associate					

Training &
Certification

Applicable to your business	HDI Cert	MCP	ITIL	Cert #1	Cert#2
Associate					
Associate					

2. Using the information from the matrix, create a graphic of your team to help you when delegating.

S-1 LEAST EXPERIENCED	S-2 MORE EXPERIENCED
S-4 MOST EXPERIENCED	S-3 EVEN MORE EXPERIENCED

S stands for skills, so assign each team member to a segment of the People Square based on the skills matrix.

The object is for your people move from one box to the next through delegation, training, coaching (by you) and their daily work.

It does take some dedicated time and concerted effort to do the initial work, but once the initial work is done, they are easy to keep up to date, although this is NOT a task that can be delegated. It is very likely that your views of where they fit and theirs aren't a match.

The payoff for this effort is enormous. The skills matrix tells you at a glance

- where the holes are, so you know what areas you need to strengthen when you hire;
- the best allocation of your training dollars;
- who to pair for cross training; and
- helps you staff your shifts.

The people square

- Is also beneficial when hiring;
- Keeps you aware of how much active managing is required; and
- Tracks your team's strengths.

USING THE SQUARE AND MATRIX WHEN DELEGATING

Frequently managers minimize the important of the soft skills in the matrix and use primarily hard skills when assigning levels; this is a huge mistake as is the opposite. Skills without the right attitude are close to worthless, whereas attitude, to a certain degree, can often compensate for skills, but you need to be aware of both.

Remember we said earlier that lower level tasks should be assigned, organized and tracked in the same way as higher–level tasks? The difference when assigning an S1 as opposed to an S4 is the amount of effort required from you.

Again, the five steps are:

1. Explain the importance and the big picture related to the tasks;
2. Assign the tasks fairly;
3. Create a cycle system to ensure tasks are assigned across the board;
4. Work with staff from other departments and train them as necessary;
5. Track small tasks in the same way you track larger ones.

People are resources and you need to spend them wisely. Although it is tempting to assign low-level tasks to S1 and complex tasks to S4, it is bad management; while it might make your life easier in the **short-term**, it would defeat the goal of team member growth, create bad feelings among the team and increase turnover in the longer term.

When attitude is equal, the major difference between delegating to an S1 and an S 4 is prep time. You will have to put more effort in the planning stage, but the tracking once the task is handed off is similar, although you may have more benchmarks and interim check-ins for the S1.

Here's a neat little trick that helps you delegate more wisely for both goals.
Divide each team member's salary by 2080 (the number of hours in a normal year).
Multiply that number by the number of hours the task will take.
The result is the **obvious** cost of delegating that task.
Now add the hidden costs.
For example, if you only assign menial tasks to S1s they are likely to quit, so you would have to add the cost of replacing that person in dollars and training time, as well as your time to repair the damage to the team's morale.

Every manager wants a team of stars. These are your go-to team members who always seem to get the task done virtually without assistance. They seem to know what you want and how to deliver it almost as if they can read your mind. Of course, this is impractical. Not only from the viewpoint of money, but there would be no way to provide the challenge and career opportunities needed to hold them

The good news is that stars are more a matter of soft skills than hard skills and the majority of stars are a result of their management. That means that your goal is to build star quality soft skills in all your team. An S1 with star quality soft skills might require more help with the hard points of planning, but beyond that initial effort, she can often equal an S2 or even an S3 with much weaker soft skills.

The greatest error managers make is not taking the time to evaluate their people so they know them well enough to delegate successfully. Trust plays an enormous role when delegating, enough that the most experienced hire will still start out as an S1 until she has earned your trust. Even then, she will move through the squares in order. Remember: you were an S1 at some point.

The other thing to remember is that sometimes people will move to a level and stay there. You're a long time S1 is still a valuable if they can accomplish the tasks you assign successfully.

Becoming expert at the fine art of delegation will pay off handsomely as your career progresses, but you can increase the payoff by always crediting your team members and not yourself. When you became a manager, your main value to the company moved from any individual effort of yours to the performance of your team.

Understanding exactly how much of your effort is required to support each of your people when delegating means that you can have a flawlessly performing team without spreading yourself too thin.

AVOIDING REVERSE DELEGATION

The amount of help people request depends on their competency.

Assuming you chose the correct person, provided all the information needed, empowered her with the authority required, approved her plan and truly handed off the project there should be little reason for her to keep asking for help.

Constant 'help me's' pave the road to reverse delegation, which means that by constantly helping you slowly end up reassuming the responsibility for the task and often end up doing much of the work.

Reverse delegation isn't always intentional or equate to your person being sneaky and trying to avoid the task. More often, it comes from her own insecurities and the desire to be safe, rather than sorry. NOTE: If your people don't feel safe making mistakes then you need to look in the mirror and correct your management style.

Here are additional techniques to handle the requests and avoid reverse delegation

- When asked for a decision, review possibilities only! Let the person take responsibility for making it.
- If the person claims she can't do the work, offer more training! Typically, there are three reasons at the bottom of 'I can't'—fear, not knowing and laziness. Training eliminates the first two leaving the third to your management skill.
- If they really cannot do the task, you are back to square one and need to go through the entire delegation process with a different team member. The responsibility for the failure is **yours**, not the other person's. You went through an entire process to avoid this, which means you either didn't use the process or were just plain sloppy. That means that the damage done to the team member is your responsibility to repair and make sure that there is no lasting effect. You can't make her a puppet and take the project back to avoid the error being noticed by your boss. Do that and you can forget about ever having any trust, respect or co-operation from the rest of the team. (Yes, they WILL know.)
- If asked to assist, instead saying you are too busy, remind her that it is her project and that you want her to accomplish it by herself. You want her to grow and be ready for bigger and better things in her career. The only way that she will be successful is by doing the work herself.

If you follow the above suggestions, it should be very easy to avoid being caught by reverse delegation.

There are two final actions involved in delegating.

1) Delegating doesn't mean that you hand off a project and forget all about it. Good delegation requires you to manage it, which means following the plan and reviewing progress, milestones and interim deadlines. **Don't delegate more than you can manage**.

2) Most importantly, and this is true in every aspect of managing, is to give praise and feedback during and at the end of the project. If you want someone to perform the same task repeatedly, you have to

show him or her you appreciate his or her efforts and approve of the work he or she is doing. Once you engage you engage your people you want them to stay engaged. We cannot restate enough the important of praise, which we discuss at more length in our Rewards and Recognition Chapter.

WHY DELEGATION FAILS

- Lack of trust.
- Incorrect or incomplete evaluation of the competencies of your team.
- Incomplete information.
- Withholding the necessary authority to do the task.
- Ignoring delegated tasks instead of managing them.

New managers often wonder what they are doing if they delegate so much. You need to understand that your position should be tactical **and** strategic in nature. This means that you need to be planning for the future of the organization and relying on your team to handle the daily operational tasks. This is especially important for the managers of smaller servicedesks where growth is eminent. Plan for the future to scale your business processes and the services you provide.

You will only be successful if you let your team do the work they need to do.

That doesn't mean that you don't roll up your sleeves, get your hands dirty and lead by example when appropriate. You don't want to work for a manager who stays in his ivory tower, nor do your people. It's worse in a smaller organization where ivory towers will lead to dissention and disengagement in your team. Stay tuned in and dig in when and how appropriate.

WHAT'S IN IT FOR ME?

You measure how your tea is doing, so we thought you would like metrics that allow you to measure just how much good delegation practices are helping you; some are quantitative, other are qualitative, both kinds are of equal value:

- Less time spent in meetings
- People on time for meetings
- Happier home life
- Enjoy work more
- Employees feel empowered and trusted
- Show management your leadership abilities
- Time
- Growth
- Efficiency and coordination
- Motivation and commitment
- Stronger interpersonal relationships

Growing as a manager means saying good-bye to Mr. Fix It. It is not a question of whether or not you are capable of doing the work—but should you?

The question to you is the same as you asked your team. Do you want to learn, grow and be fit for promotion? If so, then you need to do the things that make you promotable and one of those is delegation.

As a kind of final thought on this subject, an interesting story comes to mind. Recently, on a family trip we stopped at a Chinese Restaurant for dinner. Dinner was great and everyone was very full by the time the bill came around. With the bill, as always, were the fortune cookies.

A cookie was cracked open and the fortune read, two or three times. Whether it was divine providence or luck, my fortune read

The efficient person gets the job done right.
The effective person gets the right job done.

That's it. In this small cookie lies the wisdom that every manager needs. Everyone knows that you are an efficient person—that is why you were promoted. However, are you effective?

Are you doing the right job and are you getting your people to do the right jobs. The effective person is the manager who delegates so she can be work on the proper tasks and objectives.

Your goal is to be both efficient and effective, in essence, ensuring that the right person gets the right job done right!

CHAPTER 6. STAFFING MADE SIMPLE

We chose the title for this chapter because both authors are firm believers in the KISS model of running your work and life. If you aren't familiar with this model, we'll break it down for you. KISS stands for **K**eep **I**t **S**imple **S**tupid! What this means is that you do not need to over complicate things to get them done right. Remember, sometimes the easiest explanation is the best one to start with. Here are some easy steps for properly staffing your service desk.

Staffing is one of the more complicated tasks that any manager faces; it is also the task that affects your success the most. Our hope is to provide you some guidance into picking the staffing model that works best for you, and identifying those considerations you need to be sure not to overlook.

Certainly, in the overall makeup of a service desk, there are certain questions you are going to have to figure out before you can determine the minimum number of staff needed, let alone the distribution of those team members. Let's begin by answering some key questions.

1) What are your operating hours? This clearly has a huge impact on your staffing model, as it will not only affect the number of staff, but also their distribution.

1.1) What time zones do you support, and what time zone you are in, Where are your customers and what hours do they keep.

Considering all the above questions and their respective answers should yield the number of hours and times you will need to staff.

2) What classification of employees will you have: full-time, contractors, salaried, hourly, etc?
Knowing classifications tells you the overall availability of your staff will be.

For our example, all Service Desk employees are Regular Full Time employees with 2 weeks' vacation time, 2 personal days, 5 sick days and 10 company paid holidays. This means that in the model we will have to account for the possibility that each employee will be unavailable for the time equivalent of 27 eight-hour days.

All considerations affect your staffing budget. If you are paying overtime, but did not budget for overtime, the number of hours you have available will be seriously impacted. Ignoring particulars such as overtime pay, double time for holidays, etc., guarantees to put you over budget, possibly resulting in cutbacks and leaving you to provide the same level of service with less staff.

3) Consider the type of support you will be providing—phone, email or web support, with or without live chat or a combination.

▷ Focus on the cost per ticket, since that is a key to managing your budget.

4) Is there a Service Level Agreement (SLA) to adhere to? SLAs have significant impact on how you staff and your budget because you have a contractual obligation to furnish a specific level of service.

With or without an SLA it is imperative to determine your service level goals are going to be.

6) Metrics to measure. Beyond the SLA obligation, you need metrics against which to target, but more importantly, you need metrics to hone your staffing.

THE METRICS OF STAFFING

A few metrics are required in order to determine the minimum staff required to staff your service desk. These include:

- Mean Time to Resolve (MTTR) refers to the average time to resolve an incident
- Number of Incidents Received

Beyond these key metrics, you need to determine what other metrics that will track, report and analyze as appropriate for your business, as well as those that help you measure how you and your team are doing.

Many of the most important metrics to measure are not included in an SLA, but you need them for your team. While Customer Satisfaction and Timeliness of Resolution aren't in your SLA, they play a major role in staffing, managing your team and especially planning.

If you believe that you have enough people and are staffed at the right times, but your customers rate you 3 out of 5 for Timeliness, then you need to dig deeper to identify what is really going on. At first glance, it may look like a training issue, but with a deeper analysis, you may have found a problem that requires more resources in order to resolve it.

Employee Satisfaction is another critical metric. Both under and overstaffing will draw negative reactions, higher turnover and related staffing costs and more damage to your budget.

Staffing levels affect every single metric, whether directly or indirectly and, in turn, these metrics affect how many of your veteran employees to deploy when, one of the most significant decisions you make.

LET'S DO SOME MATH

Once you have your metrics, it is time to determine your gross staffing requirement.

The use of event tools depends on many factors (size of your team, boss' attitude, company policy, etc.) Excel works well for smaller situations; and simply Internet search on keywords, "Call Center Scheduling" will reveal a variety of off the shelf tools and services to help refine you staffing model.

In the spirit of simplicity, here is a KISS equation that should help you make intelligent decisions regarding staffing levels.

- Determine the **total number of man-hours** as opposed to the hours you are open. (X team members each working Y hours = Z man hours)

- Determine the number of work hours you are going to need to cover by multiplying the number of Incidents you receive in a year by the mean time to resolve them. (annual Incidents x MTR = work hours) OR if you sort Incidents by categories and have different MTTR's use the same formula for each category and then add the results together for the total.

The result is your Required Staffing Hours (RSH), that is, the total number of hours you need to staff to provide the acceptable level of service.

Determine Available Work Hours (AWH). Start with 2080 (40 hr/wk x 52) hours, which is the standard workweek of a full time employee.

To determine the AWH, subtract all time that takes away from working on incidents Time away (measured in hours) may include:

- Vacation Hours

- Sick Hours

- Holidays

- Breaks

- Training

- Projects

- Admin time

In short, you are saying that in a 40-hour workweek, your people do not actually spend 40 hours working incidents, emailing and taking phone calls.

The number may be closer to 30, but there is much disagreement on what this number *should* be.

The question is UTILIZATION. The theory is that Support Analyst/Service desk Agent utilization should be between 60% and 80% utilized. The reality is that those numbers are arbitrary unless you take the actual type of support into account.

Spending the entire day constantly on the phone may seem excessive, but if the reality of the job is to help people via the phone each and every day then it is realistic.

Your utilization target needs to feel right to you, but it most likely will be around the 80% mark. Factoring in vacation, sick time, training, breaks, etc, typically yields a maximum availability for each employee around 80%.

If your availability and utilization are pretty close to the same number, you are on the right track.

Next, you simply divide the RSH by the AWH and you have your gross staffing number (GSN).

The GSN is roughly the number of people you need to meet the number of incidents you have within the mean time to resolve.

To break the whole equation down, it would look something like the following:

(Incident per Year x Mean Time to Resolve) / (Potential Work Hours - Time Away) = Number of Staff You Need

Theory is great, but you function in the real world where things are not that tidy, so next you look at probable adjustments.

Is the MTTR number true and accurate? In many cases, the number generated by your incident management system may only track the amount of time from when a ticket is opened to when it is closed. You need to know whether your incident management system tells you the actual MTTR or just the time that the ticket is open.

Answer that question and you will be able to best determine your staffing requirements.

Your model also needs adjustment based upon your projected incident growth and target MTTR.

For example, your model shows you that you need 10 team members if you are solving 1000 issues a year with an MTTR of 1 week.

- If you double your customers, will you double your incidents?
- If incidents doubled, would you necessarily double the MTTR?
- If your MTTR doubles, does your staff need to do the same?
- What are the maximums your can handle with your current resources, human and otherwise?

Amazing what you can learn from a KISS staffing model.

PUTTING IT TO WORK

Now that we have gone through the theory, let's apply the simple model to our basic example. Then we'll throw in some considerations as well just to spice it up a little. First off, let's review the staffing parameters for our model.

1. All Service desk team members are Full Time* employees with these Paid Times Off:

    1. 2 Weeks Vacation

    2. 2 Personal Days

3. 5 Sick Days

4. 10 Company Holidays

*Employee classification examples: Full Time employees who get Holidays, Vacation and Sick Time? If they are, are they Hourly Paid or Salaried? Most likely on the Service Desk, and most certainly for 1st and 2nd line they will be hourly non-exempt employees and therefore eligible for Overtime. Perhaps your employees are hourly employees without benefits. Is your organization set such that they only get paid for when they work? Do you utilize contractors at all? Is it a mix of regular employees and contractors?

2. Our Service desk operates 24x7x365

3. 50% of requests come from phone an 50% come via email

4. Answer 85% of the calls within 30 seconds

5. Abandonment rate of less than 5%

6. Respond to email requests within 30 minutes

7. Six team members currently

8. Number of incidents per year 8000

9. MTTR is 8 hrs as reported by the Incident Management System

Potential Work Hours per employee is the standard 2080

Time Away is 27 days * 8 hours per day or 216 hours

The math looks like this: (8,000 x 8) / (2080 - 248) = 34 team members

This is a giant disconnect, so you need to find the discrepancy.

Most likely, it is the MTTR needing adjustment. Ask yourself:

- Is 8 hours actually the MTTR? Unlikely. If you really needed 34 people and were operating with six associates, your turnover caused by burnout would be extremely high. Depending on how you utilize your incident management system, the MTTR may represent the average time it takes to close the ticket—not to resolve the issue.

- Use your incident management system in a way that more accurately reflects the amount of time to takes to truly work the issue. Example: Assume the amount of work required is closer to 2 hours of actual dedicated work. With that small change in the equation, the number of team members would equate to 8.58 staff, or 9 full time employees, which is much closer to the 6 you actually have.

- Availability of staff.
  The equation above makes two important assumptions.
    1. Each team member takes advantage of all his or her 27 days off, and
    2. You have 100% utilization, which means that your people are always logged in whenever they are in the office leaving no time for projects, training or any other necessary time away from the desk.

- The number at which you arrive provides a better understanding of current and future staffing needs. Example: To maintain the MTTR based on the current number requires paying overtime whenever someone is out of the office. The current numbers don't allow for any breaks what so ever during the day, as well as expecting them to stay logged in 100% of the time.

- If target utilization is plus/minus 80%, you will overwork your team and increase your turnover.

What we clearly learn from this is that your current six-member team is working very hard and there are difficulties scheduling days off.

Alternately, perhaps your MTTR is not true, or fluctuates tremendously based upon staffing. You certainly don't have any room for growth in either incidents handled or improving the MTTR. Additionally, nine people are the bare minimum in terms of staffing.

Further analysis and considerations yields the following information:

Assumptions (These are **sample** assumptions and do not include staff meetings and administrative time, as well as others as appropriate to your business and culture.):

- Each employee takes 2 x 15 minute breaks each day

- Each employee has 2 hours of training time each week

- Each employee should only be 80% utilized

If we consider these numbers above, our new equation will look more like the following:

(Incident per Year x Mean Time to Resolve) / (Potential Work Hours - Time Away) = Number of Staff You Need

Time away is 27 days * 8 hours per day or 216 hours. Add another 2.5 hours each day for breaks and 2 hours a week for training. 216 hours + 4.5 hours = 220.5 hours.

The math looks like this: (8,000 x 2) / (2080 - 220.5) = 8.6 team members, or still at 9. This may look like good news, but the time for project work, administrative tasks, etc., needs to be included for your equation to be accurate.

Next, consider the 80% utilization. The utilization rate looks at the amount of time you expect your service desk staff to be actively engaged in resolution of an incident via phone, email, chat, research, etc.

The breaks during the day and 2 hours of training time accounts for 4.5 hours per week. If an employee works 40 hours a week, removing those 4.5 hours results in 88.75% utilized.

In order to give employees additional time away from incident resolution you need to increase staff by another 10% to move closer to 80% utilization. 10% * our projected nine employees means an additional 0.9 employees or one actual person, which moves you from nine full time employees to 11.

You now have a realistic number of staff to be able to ensure that people receive time off and training time, as well as preventing burn-out from being on the desk their entire day.

You also have a good basic equation to use any time you need to change projections because of an increase in incidents or a projected reduction in MTTR.

However, this only determines the number of people required to handle a projected number of incidents in a projected amount of time. You also need to consider the distribution of email vs. phone needs and the MTTR for each. With that information, you weight the model to determine how the distribution of those types of incidents might affect the number of staff needed.

Additionally, you must understand your targets for phone and response rates, because they are crucial to accurately scheduling staff.

Because the example is based on a 24x7 Service desk, those 11 people need to be assigned at different times and different days based on incident flow, which is unlikely to be evenly distributed across the week. The numbers tell you whether one person can handle the help needs during the night or you need to assign more.

IT IS CRITICAL TO CONSIDER ALL PARAMETERS AND TARGETS TO ENSURE THAT YOU DISTRIBUTE THE AVAILABLE STAFF IN THE MOST EFFECTIVE MANNER.

FOUR STAFFING RULES

1. Have a thorough understanding of your needs and targets.

2. There is a right and wrong level of staff

3. Don't assume throwing additional headcount at a problem will fix it.

4. Staff distribution must meet the needs of the specific business and company.

Remember, staffing correctly makes you look good to your boss and your team, so take the time to learn to do it right.

CHAPTER 7. BUILDING STRONG TEAMS

Assuming that you live and work in this Universe you have heard about the importance of having a strong team.

A group does not constitute a team; nor is a minimum number of people required.

A team comprises a group of people linked in a common purpose. The best teams have members with complementary skills and generate synergy through a coordinated effort that allows members to maximize their strengths and minimize their weaknesses. A team works together towards a common purpose and their skills are required to function in unison to complete the task.

If a team is linked by common purpose then team building includes

      (a) Clarifying the goal and building ownership across the team;
      (b) Identifying the inhibitors to teamwork; and
      (c) Mitigating their negative effect on the team, including removal from it.

Your job as manager is to engage in activities that ensure the members of the team understand the specified goal and work towards removing any obstacles that may prevent achieving it.

Challenges abound whether you are building a large team or a smaller one. With larger teams, in addition to the standard management headaches, there are increased logistical issues when scheduling, far more disparate personalities, more opportunities to play politics, etc.

Smaller teams face the reality that one team member who isn't working towards the shared vision has far more disruptive power and does more damage faster. Worse, as people notice, they will start to exclude that person; decisions are made without her input further reducing engagement; the cycle keeps repeating further alienating both sides and tearing the team apart.

As with disengagement, a single voice of dissent will have a much larger impact. This does not mean that team members should always agree, but the same person constantly disagreeing is less easily ignored in a group of four than 50.

TWO WAYS TO BUILD A TEAM

With a basic understanding of what a team is and why we might have team building exercises, it is time to tackle a very large myth of team building. The idea that forcing your team to have dinner together is team building is simply a fallacy. Don't get caught up in thinking that ordering a pizza for the office is team building. While we are not condemning the act of feeding your employees, don't be mistaken that giving away free food to a group of people in the same area is team building.

There are two distinct types of team building, goal-based and just-for-fun, and they work best when **both** are used.

Whichever you choose, be prepared for statements such as, *"I know why we are doing this,"* or *"This is so corny."* For a variety of reasons, some people just aren't comfortable with team building exercises, especially the physical ones.

If this happens, take the person aside, discuss the reaction privately, and help him get comfortable with doing it.

In some cases, there can be a valid physical reason, such as being out-of-shape or a heart condition, or psychological one, such as fear of heights, which prevents him from wanting to participate. Minimizing, ridiculing, or embarrassing him in front of the team won't accomplish anything, whereas an honest discussion that respects his feelings will go a long way to building trust and resolving the situation. If the reason is real, then you may want to consider using a different exercise or finding a way for him to participate differently.

Goal Based Team Building

Goal based team-building focuses on one specific goal. It can either be stated up front or taught at the conclusion of the exercise, much like the moral of a story.

There are many kinds of goal-based exercises, from the simple to the extreme. They range from a brainstorming session to write the department's mission statement to a ropes course designed to build trust.

The key to success lies in the fact that the exercise leader, whether that be you as the manager or someone else, knows exactly what the goal is **before** the exercise begins. You can't wing it or change it after the fact—your team will know, trust will be reduced and your authenticity will take a major hit. You need to prepare, know exactly why you are doing the exercise, what you want to accomplish and be ready to discuss openly the results and how they affect the dynamic of the team.

Decide whether to state the goal up-front or at the end based on what you want to accomplish. In some cases, the lesson learned is more powerful when the explanation of the goal comes at the end. Explain the goal at the start when you will be referencing it throughout the exercise.

Just Fun Team Building

Just fun team building focuses on improving relationships. Relationships are the basis for our lives. All your activities revolve around relationships, whether with your family, friends, co-workers, service desks, retailers, etc. You can't avoid them—relationships are everywhere.

Because fun events focus on relationship building, it helps when you use ways in which your team gets to know each other away from the office and the pressures of the customer.

Even fun exercises should be guided, with a definite goal in mind.

Venting together can be turned from a negative dumping into a positive coming together if you add a "solve or neutralize" component. You do this by having one person rant and then everyone brainstorming ways to get over/through/around the problem. They can be serious, silly or even outrageous, the goal is to share laughter and diminish the effect of the irritant.

Sometimes a serious problem will be uncovered during a rant; one that is a molehill just waiting to become a mountain. When that happens, ask everyone to think about ways to address it and schedule a time to meet and resolve it.

Eating together is always good. Whether you take your people out or order pizza in, eat together and get to know each other. Avoid talking business. If the conversation lags, suggest one of many verbal games; if the conversation is dominated by a topic that does not engage everyone, gently steer it in another direction.

If your desk runs 24/7, whether large or small, it is almost impossible to find a time for the whole team to get together. In that case, ordering in, rotating people and having more than one event usually works well.

Just Fun team building exercises are excellent when the unstated goal is bonding. These can be everything from pickup basketball to organized off-site events that include families.

Family events don't have to be expensive. BBQs in the parking lot and potlucks are great socializers. Bringing families together puts names to faces; it lets spouses meet the people their partners spend nearly half their time with; kids meet and often become friends.

The more comfortable your employees are around each other, the more vested they be in their colleagues and productivity will rise.

Not all people are comfortable socializing with their workmates, so when the event is on their own time you shouldn't use coercion techniques to force them. Rather you need to learn why someone doesn't want to participate. Is it scheduling, family commitment, or no interest in the activity? Be willing to work around these problems by creating events that circumvent or avoid them.

Will you have a problem if their reluctance remains? That depends on the individual. Some are so standoffish that it can increase stress and lower productivity (why did you hire them), while others are just very private people who prefer to keep work and personal life totally separate, but play well with the team during work hours.

HOW TO BUILD YOUR TEAM

In many ways **you** don't build it, you facilitate the process by providing activities that encourage your people to build relationships.

Here are four guidelines to help you

1) **Know your finances.** – Always set the team building budget at the start of your company's fiscal year (usually January). Team building should be a separate line item from rewards and recognition in the budget. Knowing how much money you have in total means you can plan events all year instead of using it all first quarter.

2) **Don't reinvent the wheel!** – Instead of racking your brain dreaming up goal based and just fun activities, check out the wealth of ideas in books, videos, websites, etc. Be sure to take advantage of your company's internal resources, from event planners and HR to managers with teams you would like to imitate.

3) **ASK your team!** – Rather than choosing **your** favorite activities, give them the event parameters, including cost, and let them create something that they really **want** to do.

4) **Pizza is good,** but it should be your backup, not your whole act.

There are as many different ways to promote both Goal Based and Just Fun team building as there are people who think about it; you'll find more ideas and sources in the Reference section at the end of the book.

The key to successful team building is never lose track of the money, especially exercises done on non-company time. Know ahead of time who is going to pay and recognize that expecting people to pay for the privilege of spending their own time with their business colleagues instead of with family and friends or just chilling will not be a popular idea.

Finally, be sure to keep track of what the team likes and doesn't like, that way you can repeat the good and avoid the bad.

For more ideas and resources to help you implement a great team-building program, be sure to check out the References, Ideas, and Suggestions and at end of the book.

CHAPTER 8. APPRAISALS

First, a short trip down memory lane...

You are back in High School. It's senior year and everything is great. You are taking Physical Education because it is required to graduate. You are told at the beginning of the school year that you have to get at least a "C" to graduate and go on to college.

You spend the next nine months working your butt off in dodge ball, kick ball, softball, square dancing, basketball, volleyball and every other activity your Phys Ed teacher assigns.

Just as the year ends you receive a call from the guidance counselor who sadly says that you will not be graduating because you failed to pass Gym Class.

"What the ^$&%#!" you scream after picking yourself up off the floor. **"Why didn't anyone tell me?"**

Avoiding this scenario is why schools furnish students with interim reviews and grades called report cards each semester. Students are well aware of how they are doing, whether or not they are achieving their required goals and learn well in advance if they are in a potentially risky position.

Appraisals are report cards for grownups.

EVERYONE NEEDS A LITTLE DIRECTION!

People dread the appraisal process; managers don't like to give them and workers don't enjoy receiving them. But it doesn't have to be that way.

Done correctly, appraisals/reviews are one of your best tools in employee retention and growth. More importantly, appraisals are the cornerstone of developing a highly effective and productive set of individuals to form your high performing team.

Your organization has a set process for performing appraisals; be sure to learn that process, because you need to conform to the company standards set by HR.

In addition to complying with your company's appraisal process, we believe you can take a more creative, positive approach and avoid the trap of an empty focus on meeting the documentation requirements.

Here is a simple process for enriching your basic company appraisal:

Step 1: Plan

This step is as simple as letting everyone know when you are planning to perform the appraisals. Whether or not your company sets the schedule, make sure your employees are well prepared. If part of the process includes self-assessment give them plenty of time, since this is something with which many of us struggle; they need enough time to fill out the form as completely, thoroughly and honestly as possible.

Step 2: Do the Appraisal

The appraisal is an important step. At one time or another you have probably worked for an organization that had all kinds of appraisal processes in place, but were never done. HR didn't to care and it became a running joke.

It is frustrating to be in a job for several years and not be reviewed by your manager—no objectives, no direction, no knowledge of how well you are doing.

Or the opposite, where your yearly review was completed on time, signed off and filed away in your permanent record—also with no objectives, direction or knowledge of how well you were doing. In this case, the appraisal process seems to be more a matter of form than a system designed to improve you or a team member.

But now you have a choice. You may choose to be the kind of manager described above or you can utilize the appraisal process to truly build competent team members.

Step 3: DO THE APPRAISAL

It may seem as if we are repeating ourselves, but in this email/texting world capital letters clearly mean we are yelling in an effort to get our point across. Steps 2 and 3 are the difference between hearing and listening.

Step 2 is filling out the paperwork and sitting down with your employee.

Step 3 is having a stake in the results and outcome of the process (keep in mind that your own review and compensation depends on your team's performance) and making sure your people know it.

We believe the following tips will enable you and your team to get the most out of reviews no matter what process your organization uses.

GETTING STARTED

Have a discussion at the beginning of each appraisal with of your people. Explain that the entire appraisal process is designed to help her improve and revolves around positive reinforcement.

It is not a witch-hunt or a means to get rid of someone. If you have a team member who is not a good fit or not pulling their weight, the appraisal process is not an excuse to get rid of them; you need to address those issues head on outside of the review cycle.

Reviews are about the individual, how she can improve and add more value to herself, the team and the company.

SCORING!

All reviews have a section in which you rate team members and it is critical that you understand what the scale means and how to apply it.

It might be a number from 1 to 5, or perhaps a rating system from Completely Unsatisfactory to Completely Satisfactory. You may even encounter the Does Not Meet Expectations vs. Always Exceeds Expectations. Just be sure you have a clear definition for, and understanding of, each score you assign.

The scoring section is a great time to set the review tone. Explain how the scale works and what the scores mean. Most importantly, explain that reaching top scores or perfect marks is supposed to be very hard.

If you have an employee who hit top scores for everything all the time they are not being challenged. They have probably outgrown their position and should be moved to a new one with added responsibility or they will get bored and leave.

It is important for employees to understand that the appraisal and scores section is a profile of current work efforts and, more importantly, a way to help identify areas to improve, which increases their professional value.

OBJECTIVES

An objective is a combination or series of tasks focused on meeting a specific business need or personal development goal.

When setting objectives for your people you must be sure they are realistic and agreed upon by each individual. Although some objectives are just part of the job; people become far more vested in their work when they feel in control and a part of the decision making process.

If you use self-appraisals, suggest that they include their thoughts on what their objectives should be and are currently. This lays the groundwork for a good conversation ending with mutual agreement.

When it comes time to review progress both you and your people will feel that this is something you have put together as a team.

Typically, people can only manage three to five main objectives at a time; too many objectives sets them up to fail and it will be your responsibility for not correctly managing their workload.

Be sure everybody understands that it is their responsibility to come to you before appraisal time if there are resources, time or financial reasons they are not achieving, or at least progressing, on their objectives.

Objectives are dependent on your business needs and must be designed accordingly. People aren't stupid; they know when the objectives are outside of your business or just plain busy work and will react negatively.

Objectives should play to employees' strengths and of interest to them, although at times you will have to assign an objective that is not a favorite task, but that is just the nature of work. That is why discussion and agreement is so important.

Examples of goals or objectives for a service desk:

- Building a Business Continuity Plan for your Service Desk
- Writing 10 knowledgebase articles each month
- Improving the Self Service portion of the Customer Portal
- Creating a Tag Line for your Support department
- Submitting an article to a trade journal (This is great for industry recognition.)
- Speaking at a local professional organization meeting (An excellent way to help your employees' network and improve the visibility of your company.)
- Documenting specific processes
- Creating a training manual

ACTION PLANS

Depending on your specific appraisal process and forms you may or may not encounter action plans, but you do need an action plan. It doesn't need to be complicated, should reflect the different levels of your people and be a joint effort, as were the objectives. The plan has mutually agreed upon steps to ensure that each of you knows exactly what needs to occur to ensure the goals are reached.

A major part of developing an action plan is establishing the main milestones and detailing any supporting materials or resources that may be needed.

AN ACTION PLAN BASED ON THE OBJECTIVES EXAMPLE ABOVE:

GOAL / OBJECTIVE	ACTION PLAN
Building a Business Continuity Plan for your Service Desk	• Document Business Continuity Steps in the Event of a Disaster • Plan training drills • Create audit sheet to track training drills • Create a list of required resources (Cell Phone, Wi-Fi Card for Laptop, Etc) • Create copies of plan and distribute to appropriate personnel
Writing 10 Knowledgebase Articles Each Month	• Compose articles based upon existing or new processes or on technical assistance articles • Update existing articles that have become dated
Submitting an article to a trade journal (This is great for industry recognition)	• Compose an article on a topic of interest to you • Generate a list of target magazines and trade journals • Submit article for printing

It is imperative to explain to your team that *you* are not responsible for them meeting their goals—they are. You will facilitate, but it is not acceptable for any reason to come back at the next appraisal and say they didn't do anything Drive home the understanding that you will provide the time, financial and resource assistance they require, but they are responsible for requesting it as appropriate.

This is one of the most important aspects of this process. Your self-starters will take this as a challenge and want to achieve their goals ahead of schedule. They will take notes and write down additional action plan items and ideas to help them progress; others may not respond as positively, but keep in mind that they may only have experienced the type of reviews we described at the start of this chapter and are not expecting anything different.

SKILLS

A skill is a proficiency that is acquired or developed through training or experience.

If your company's appraisal process does not have a skills section it is a good idea to add one that documents the specific skills that you both agree are crucial to success in the position.

Having a robust set of skills is important for everyone, no matter their position; having a set skills target is a perfect way to help them develop into their next role and give them goals for which to strive. This is especially helpful when people ask what they have to do for a promotion or to reach the next level.

One of your best tools for skills development is a skills matrix. The skills matrix you created for delegating focused on your teams current skills, where as this one will help identify the specific skills you need to have a well-rounded team.

Combining the information in the delegating matrix with the skills needed helps you set goals for each team members based on weak areas.

Creating a skills matrix is simple; just outline what skills are required to accomplish your service desk's work. The following example includes only the basics, so add any others that apply to your company and business:

SKILLS MATRIX

Legend

0 = No skill

1 – Beginning

2 – Intermediate

3 – Expert

TECHNICAL

Applicable to your business	Skill 1	Skill 2	Skill 3	Skill 4	Skill 5
Associate					
Associate					

Skill Level Average (Target 2.3)

PROFESSIONAL SOFT SKILLS

Applicable to your business	Time Management	Prioritization	Teamwork	Phone	Technical Writing
Associate					
Associate					

Skill Level (Target 2.3)

Next, determine a rating scale and list all your team members. You may score them or let them score themselves. You can create an average skill rating and even set a target average.

This means that if SQL skills are extremely important and your current average skill rating is 1.4 when it should be closer to 3 (Expert according to the scale above), then you clearly need to focus one or more team members on improving their SQL skills.

The skills matrix is a living breathing document. As your business changes and your team grows the required skills may change as well, so be sure set a regular schedule to update the matrix to be sure that your team is working towards timely and required goals.

As with objectives, limit the number of developing skills to between three and five during any appraisal period. Your people are responding to emails, web tickets and phone calls; you don't want to overload them; since some skills are easier to master assign improvement based upon your judgment of workload and the ability of each team member.

Although your focus for skills development is to fill the gaps in your team's overall skill set, your people are focused on improving their skills and being promoted or changing jobs. Those who want a career in Customer Service and the Service Desk need to build skills that keep them in the field; others see the Service Desk as a stepping-stone to some other career, but that may change if they develop appropriate skills.

Your opportunity to stand out as a manager is what you do with the appraisal process beyond filling out HR's forms. Let's start with this concept:

"AN APPRAISAL IS A CONTRACT BETWEEN TWO PARTIES, MANAGER AND EMPLOYEE, WHEREBY BOTH ARE RESPONSIBLE FOR THEIR PART OF THE DEAL."

KEYS TO EXCELLENT REVIEWS

- If you assign objectives, but do not provide everything the person needs to achieve them, then the fault is YOURS; however, once you both agree if they do not ask/remind you then the fault is THEIRS.
- Appraisals are a way to encourage and evaluate progress, NOT a process by which to find fault or cull the team.
- Reviews require open communications, set expectations and joint agreement in order to succeed.
- The appraisal process is a two-way street requiring discussion of the forms, objectives, skills development and targets.
- Never have more than three to five objectives and three to five skills improvements in any appraisal period; the exact number is adjusted for each person.
- When the appraisal is finished, review and discuss it to ensure that the team member understands it and agrees with the objectives.
- Provide a copy of the final, signed review to the employee for her files.
- Whether or not your company's process provides a copy of the final document for the employee, you should provide them with it.
- The final review is a contract that requires both of you to live up to its terms.

The last Key provides you with a great opportunity to drive home the on-going value of the appraisal. Remind them the review is meant to serve as a guide over the next year.

Suggest they print it out, leave a copy on their desk, review it daily and enter individual objectives as Tasks or Calendar items.

ADDITIONAL TIPS FOR YOUR MANAGERIAL TOOLBOX

Tip 1. There is one more benefit for doing excellent reviews—and it is yours.

Formal paperwork comes only once a year, but putting an informal 'how am I doing' review process in place helps keep them on track and assures them of your interest in their success.

The frequency of informal reviews is dependent on the size of your team and your own workload, but whatever you do the key to them working is consistency.

With or without paperwork; formally or informally; monthly, quarterly, bi-annually; the important idea is to provide constant feedback, so your people know how they are doing and what still needs to be done to achieve their goals.

The idea of continual improvement is a theme throughout the book and one that is impossible unless you are always reviewing where you stand.

As with everything else, some employees need more checkups and others fewer, but the critical point is that there are no surprises at the next annual review.

Tip 2. Create a scorecard for your team.

This may already exist within your organization, but might need modification. The scorecard is simply a spreadsheet for each employee that looks at measurable components of their job.

Look at your objectives, tactical and strategic targets and define a scorecard based on those.

Example; Measurements might include

- Customer Satisfaction Score
- Survey's Received
- Average Talk Time
- Average Time to Abandon
- Unplanned Absences

Fill out a scorecard for each employee monthly or quarterly depending on the size of your team and your business. Scorecards are based on fact, not opinion, so this is a great opportunity to get supervisors and team leads involved. Breaking up the work makes it much easier on you and gives you an opportunity to train future managers.

After each period the scorecards are filled out, schedule a brief meeting with each team member to review their scorecard. This meeting is probably no more than 5 minutes. It provides constant feedback to your employees and ensures they are always on track. For instance, if someone seems to have many unplanned absences over a three-month period, it may be a sign of an issue. You can address it at the end of the month 3 rather than waiting until the end of the year. The same would hold true for low customer satisfaction scores. The idea is that you can react in near time to what is happening with your employees and stop any issues before they get worse or lead to a situation where you have to consider termination. The scorecard process also ensures that each of your team members gets a little face time with you one-on-one each period, which can always come in handy. It shows that you are interested in their well-being and are ready to talk to them. Use it as a nice chance to ask them how they are doing and how's the job going. When you have employees working second and third shift this is especially helpful as you may not see them all that much, but this reminds them that you are around.

Never forget that your goal is for appraisals to be an opportunity for your employees. With proper establishment of goals and targets, you can use the process to develop the best possible team and team members. Armed with your skills matrix, scorecards and informal appraisal process you can be constantly engaged with your team's development and, more importantly, viewed by them as a staunch supporter of their efforts.

CHAPTER 9. METRICS THAT MATTER,
NO MATTER YOUR SIZE

ONE OF THE RARE FEW ITEMS WE DEAL WITH WHICH ARE ABSOLUTE. AND INARGUABLE ARE OUR METRICS

Metrics are numbers—statistics—and the beauty of statistics is that they don't lie. How one interprets those data is another story altogether.

Before we go into which are the most important metrics for a service desk manager let's look at some metrics myths.

METRICS MYTHS—TRUE OR FALSE?

Myth #1) Small service desks don't need metrics!

Myth Revealed: False! ALL service desks need metrics regardless of size. The size of your group has nothing to do with your need to analyze their productivity and efficiency.

Myth #2) First Call Resolution (FCR) is the most important metric!

Myth Revealed: False! "Most important" is situation sensitive and depends completely on your business model AND your company's attitude.

Myth #3) FCR should be 80%!

Myth Revealed: False! ITIL has taught us that the business dictates their technology requirements and **metrics follow that same rule**.

Myth #4) Abandon Rate

Myth Revealed: False! The value of the abandon rate metric has been steadily declining with the rise of automated menus and the trend to push customers towards email and web ticketing. It is also more difficult to measure accurately due to ACD systems and IVR's that delay calls and reduces the chance for it to be answered.

Myth #5) Mean Time to Resolution (MTTR)

Myth Revealed: False! While MTTR is important, especially when staffing (as discussed earlier) and its statistics are also subject to the business model, types of customers and the methods used to field those issues. Far worse, the MTTR can be easily manipulated. By closing issues early without completing the work, you can manipulate the Closure vs. Resolution and make the numbers look good. However, this is a very stupid thing to do considering the giant impact MTTR has on staffing.

THE MOST IMPORTANT METRIC

The most important metric isn't a metric, it's a **shape.**

We proudly present the one and only thing you need ever know when it comes to metrics—a metrics triangle**.**

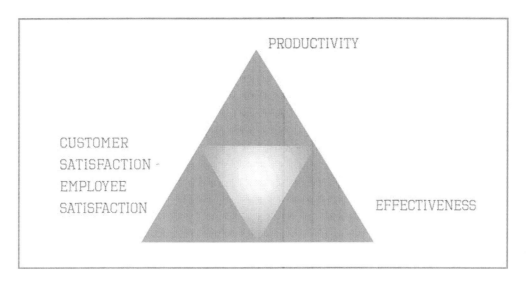

A metrics triangle does not have any specific metrics; rather it shows the different groupings or types of measurements on which to focus to give yourself a balanced view of your organization.

The three areas are as follows:

Productivity - These metrics will give you an understanding of exactly how much is being done by your team and/or organization.

Effectiveness - This will tell you how efficient your team or organization is at providing services to your customers

Customer Satisfaction/Employee Satisfaction - If you are using customer satisfaction you look at metrics that tell you how likely your customers are to return for more service. If you use Employee Satisfaction, you look at the retention rate, AKA employee longevity. On the other hand, you can combine both for an overall satisfaction measurement.

NO SINGLE METRIC IS MORE POWERFUL THAN A METRICS TRIANGLE ITSELF.
A METRICS TRIANGLE

Why a triangle? Because an equilateral triangle is not only one of the most perfect shapes, but also one of the strongest—force applied to any one side only makes the opposing sides stronger and the force is repelled.

Further, being equilateral enforces the idea that you must take a balanced approach to the data you present. Focus too much on one area means you lose balance and end up with a weaker structure; you fix it by refocusing on the areas you have ignored.

Always strive for an equilateral triangle, because then you will achieve a perfect balance in how you evaluate your team.

The balanced scorecard approach to business is one model used to ensure that quality management is achieved in the workplace. We developed our own balanced scorecard model specifically for service desks.

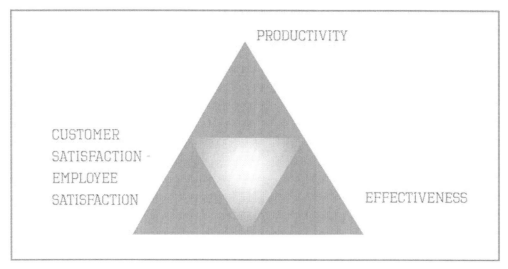

Looking at the two together you can easily see how the scorecard feeds the desired measurement areas in a metrics triangle and how **changing one metric will impact the others**.

Both support the idea of a balanced approach in everything you do—business, the service desk, your life.

A METRICS TRIANGLE IN DETAIL

Productivity

The four metrics we rejected earlier as most important do go together to supply the productivity metrics. You may add additional measurements or drop one in order to tweak the information so it is a perfect fit for **your** service desk, company and business.

- **MTTR (Mean Time to Resolve)** - You can look at MTTR by different types, such as Category, Severity, etc. You can use MTTR as a measure of Effectiveness as well as Productivity, but you **cannot use both in the same metrics triangle**.
- **Number of Incidents** - This is the most popular metric; what is the raw amount of work being performed by your team. Incidents, tickets or whatever term you use gives you a basic understanding of the total workload. Additionally, you can break this down by channel, or source, etc.
- **Abandon Rate** - Knowing how often customers hang up before receiving service gives productivity insight as well. If you take 100 calls a day, but your abandon rate is 40%, then you are not as productive as the Number of Incidents makes you sound. As with MTTR, you can also use Abandon Rate to look at efficiency, but again, **you cannot use both in the same metrics triangle.**
- **Financial Metrics -** Cost per Ticket and Cost per Contract have a direct relationship to number of incidents handled, so they are useful in determining productivity. Each of these measure quantity and should be considered when making changes to your team, process or procedures. While reducing costs may be a goal, a metrics triangle allows you to see how that affects the other measurements of interest.

Effectiveness

As we move clockwise in a metrics triangle the next criteria we come to is Effectiveness. As with Productivity, there are many different measurements from which to select. Here are the seven most often used, but be sure to customize them for your own situation:

- **FCR (First Contact Resolution)** – Although a high FCR rate seems optimal, its value is substantially lessened when paired with a high Re-Open rate, which indicates that the information your customers are receiving is not solving their problems.

- **Re-Opened Incident Rate** – A high Re-Open rate usually indicates a lack of Effectiveness because the problem was not properly resolved the first time.

- **Hierarchical Escalations** - Hierarchical Escalations occur when a problem is passed up to a supervisor or manager because the team member can't approve the solution, doesn't know the answer or the customer requests it. Escalation is a good indicator regarding training needs and whether your team has the authority to provide efficient assistance to your customers.

- **Technical Escalations** - Effectiveness is also impacted by how often your analysts need to refer up to 2nd or 3rd level or even a different horizontal resource to get assistance. However, the rate is tied to how your company has structured knowledge levels within its support area.

- **Resolution Time Distribution** - One of the best ways to measure your Effectiveness is by analyzing when the majority of your tickets are resolved. The analysis can explain a deviation of the MTTR and indicate where to make adjustments. In the same way, you can look at what percentage of time you are meeting your SLA, when you miss it, how far off you are, and then adjust accordingly.

- **Self-Help Use** - Self-service is cheaper for the business and potentially faster for the customer, while reducing overwork and stress. By measuring frequency of use, you rate its effectiveness and determine how to improve it so your customers will make better use of it.

- **Backlog Management** - Although backlog is business-model dependent, it still needs to be managed. Combining backlog numbers with other metrics will yield the true information about your operations enabling you to make better tactical decisions.

Customer and Employee Satisfaction

While the other two thirds of a metrics triangle look at what you are doing and how well you do it, the satisfaction metrics focus on the business needs of revenue and retention. Here is a sampling of useful metrics, but, as always, you must adjust them for you own situation.

Customer Satisfaction

- **Periodic Customer Satisfaction** - As you probably know, there are different types of customer satisfaction measurements. The first is a Periodic Customer Satisfaction Survey and it is your overall barometer for the support you provide. This is a survey that is usually sent out 1 to 2 times per year and just asks the customers how they feel about the overall support your organization provides. The questions will be broad and you are trying to get an overall opinion rather than feedback on specific incidents that may have occurred.

- **Event-Based Customer Satisfaction** - Unlike the Periodic Survey, your event-based survey will be looking for scores and metrics for specific incidents handled by your service desk. This type of survey will have much more of an ebb and flow than the periodic, as it can be difficult to provide 100% survey 100% of the time. People make mistakes and this survey will help catch those errors allowing you to train and mentor your team. This type of survey also provides you feedback as to who your stars are, as well as which team members may that need extra assistance.

- **Feedback Metrics** - Performing some type of survey is a great start, but it is only a start. It is what you do with that feedback that will tell your customers whether or not you are listening. To that end, it is important to respond to the feedback you receive and let the customer know how you use the information to make improvements or award your team members. This will not only show your commitment to continual improvement, but also encourage your customers to continue to respond to surveys because they will see you actively utilizing the feedback. With that in mind, one simple metric you can measure to help you understand your feedback processes would be the percentage of Surveys that require Feedback and your Response rate to those. Another metric to use is how quickly you are responding to surveys. For instance, responding to feedback is great, but if your average response time to survey feedback is 30 days, your customers may not think you are taking their feedback as seriously as if you respond within 48 hours.

Employee Satisfaction
- **Overall Employee Satisfaction** - Like Customer Satisfaction, you should be concerned about Employee Satisfaction as well. We all know the saying that happy employees are productive employees, right? Well in the case of customer service, unhappy employees make for unhappy customers. Customers can hear and feel when the person responding to their issue isn't "in to" the job and this is especially true when dealing with phone support. In the case of the smaller service desk, you need to consider that your customers and team members probably know each other quite well. In this case, the customers may sense when someone is having a bad day because they know what to expect of the conversation or interaction. Measure your employee satisfaction periodically and ensure that you address the results in your meetings and have action items where you can show progress. Again, the Triangle makes us remember that even when the FCR is 90% if your employee satisfaction is only 20% the FCR won't stay high for long.

- **Unexpected Absence** - A simple metric you can measure that may be indicative of a problem. When people aren't happy at work or are stressed out, we see an increase in sick time being used. Tracking this overtime can identify serious problems ranging from family difficulties to dislike of the job.

- **Employee Turnover** - The ultimate measure of Employee Satisfaction is going to be your turnover rate. You can measure this several different ways, including expected, desired, unexpected, etc. You just need to define your goals before you start to measure. Looking at the percentage of team members who leave to work somewhere else is indicative of whether you are running a good organization or not. No matter the size of your organization turnover is very serious. However, setting your goal at 0% turnover, meaning nobody leaves, is probably unreasonable. Some things are simply out of your control, so give yourself a break and set realistic goals.

We stressed earlier that the strength of a metrics triangle comes from the balanced approach that makes it an equilateral triangle—one of the strongest shape in nature.

A metrics triangle draws its power, as does the Project Management Triangle, by forcing you to take a balanced approach and not focus on one area to the detriment of the others.

Not surprisingly, this is what many companies and managers have problems doing.

There is a Cost vs. Benefit for everything we do in business. This is no different when we look at how we decide what metrics shape our business decisions and define our strategies. A metrics triangle is about maintaining balance in how your measure and then manage your organization. By having a balanced approach you will make better decisions.

One major insight you should gain from all this is that **there is no silver bullet** when it comes to measuring your team.

A second is that a balanced approach using a variety of metrics in a metrics triangle is the best way to manage your team.

Another is that metrics are just numbers; simply a tool. 10 pages of daily metrics do not add value just because you have them. Part of your job, and your value, is identifying which metrics work, which to dump and how to use them to build a stronger team and achieve happier customers. Often a simple one-page report consisting of four or five charts and some explanations is your most powerful tool when explaining to management or your team what/how you are doing.

4 RULES TO REMEMBER ABOUT METRICS

1. METRICS ARE A MEANS, NOT AN END.
2. <u>METRICS HELP YOU IDENTIFY YOUR PROBLEMS AND INEFFICIENCIES.</u>
3. METRICS SHOW YOU WHAT YOU DO WELL AND WHERE TO PUT YOUR EFFORT.
4. A METRICS TRIANGLE KEEPS YOU BALANCED.

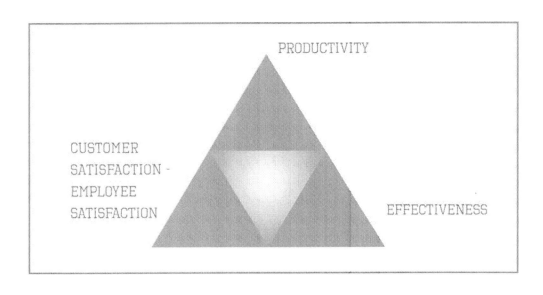

CHAPTER 10.

IT SERVICE MANAGEMENT 101

In the simplest terms, IT Service Management (ITSM) is about maximizing the value that the IT organization delivers to the business. At its core, ITSM is customer-centric; operating on the principle that IT delivers services to enable the business to achieve desired outcomes. In contrast with conventional technology-centric approaches to IT management, ITSM requires the IT organization to focus on the relationship with the customer and the quality of service provision.

While there are a plethora of standards and frameworks from which to choose, without doubt, the most popular and widely adopted framework is the IT Infrastructure Library® (ITIL®). Although the remainder of this chapter is primarily focused on ITIL®, it should be noted that there are many parallels with other frameworks and the advice given later in this chapter can be applied to other frameworks that support ITSM.

A BRIEF HISTORY OF ITIL®

In 1986, a UK Government body, the Central Computer and Telecommunications Agency (CCTA) authorized a program to develop a common set of operational guidance with the objective of increasing quality and efficiency in UK Government IT. In 1989 the first book was published, followed other publications that grew ITIL® v1 to over 30 volumes during the early 90's.

In 2000, the CCTA became part of the UK Office of Government Commerce (OGC) and during 2001 ITIL® v2 was published. To make ITIL® v2 more concise and useable, related IT management disciplines were logically grouped into a collection of eight books. However, practitioners mainly focused on the Service Support and Service Delivery publications (aka, the Blue and Red books).

By the mid-2000's, ITIL® v2 was certainly popular in Europe and adoption across North America and the Asia Pacific regions was increasing. The framework was relatively simple, with familiar processes that could easily be understood by IT personnel. There was no defined starting point, so virtually any process could be adopted first, enabling IT organizations to address the areas where they felt the most pain. However, critics complained about the lack of 'how-to' examples and felt that v2 was too concerned with IT organizing itself around processes, which often didn't translate into business value. IT sometimes struggled to make a business case for adoption, as return on investment could be difficult to demonstrate and was mainly focused on reducing IT costs and minimizing downtime.

After much aplomb and anticipation, ITIL® v3 was released to a waiting audience in May 2007. The core ITIL® v2 processes; Incident, Problem, Change, Release etc. remained largely intact in ITIL® v3 and although new processes and concepts were introduced, their roots could be found in the previous version. Components such as Service Catalog, previously buried in the ITIL® v2 material, were brought to the fore and the concepts were better explained. Now that v3 has celebrated its fourth birthday, like any toddler, much has been learned in the early years.

An update to ITIL® v3 was announced during 2009 and after 18 months work, the new ITIL® volumes were released on July 29, 2011. This update rebrands ITIL® v3 as ITIL® 2011 and addresses some inconsistencies in the ITIL® v3 (2007) books. The much critiqued ITIL® 2007 Service Strategy book (264 pages) has been reviewed and the ITIL® 2011 version now weighs in at 469 pages, with revised diagrams that seek to explain the concepts in a clearer and more accessible manner.

The ITIL® 2011 publications maintain the purity of ITIL® v3 concepts and a similar structure has been used across the publications to improve consistency and navigation. It wouldn't be possible to describe ITIL® within a single chapter, but for those that are new to the framework, here's a very brief description of the ITIL® Service Lifecycle and its phases.

ITIL® AND THE SERVICE LIFECYCLE

The introduction of the Service Lifecycle within ITIL® v3 reflected a departure from a process-centric view of IT and a move towards IT Services defined from a business perspective. The Service Lifecycle offered a holistic approach, spanning 'cradle to grave' management of services and each of the ITIL® core volumes covers its phases.

The core ITIL® volumes

The ITIL® books start with Service Strategy, where the market, resources and capabilities of IT Service Management are defined, and the overall business objectives for IT Services are established. Guidance is provided on defining, developing and implementing service management, so that the service provider can prioritize investment in services. The market driven approach encourages the service provider to stop and think **_why_** something has to be done, before working out **_how_** to do it.

Service Design focuses on turning strategy into reality, providing guidance on the design and development of services and processes. The primary objective of Service Design is to ensure that IT Services deliver what the business needs, and that management systems, tools, supporting architecture, processes and relevant metrics are considered in the design phase.

Service Transition spans the gap between projects and operations, minimizing risk and improving quality by ensuring that new or changed services are properly scoped, built and tested before delivery into operation.

Service Operation manages the effective and efficient provision of support for Services in the production environment. This is where 'the rubber meets the road' and this practical experience of service delivery is used to provide feedback to the other stages of the Service Lifecycle.

As the name suggests, Continual Service Improvement (CSI) manages the improvement process, evolving IT Services to meet changing business needs and providing input to the other phases to drive improvement across the lifecycle.

Immediately after its 2007 release, ITIL® v3 received much praise for the introduction of the Service Lifecycle approach, which promised to clarify the relationship between IT Services and the business processes they support. ITIL® 2011 provides further clarification around how services add and realize value. Business relationship management is added as a process and a role to further map the path for integration of IT with business goals at a strategic level through communication with the business. The ITIL® 2011 framework also describes ways that IT can deliver services to the business on time and within budget.

ITIL® – THE REALITIES OF ADOPTION

The ITIL® framework is often described as 'documented common sense' and an opportunity to learn from the experiences of others. The guidance contained within the core volumes has helped many IT organizations improve service quality and operational efficiency. However, research shows that even years after its release, adoption of the more strategic and proactive ITIL® disciplines remains limited. Although the concepts of ITIL® are sound and should radically improve communication with the business, there is a sense that many practitioners struggle with how much of it they can apply today, to really make a difference to the quality of IT Services.

In 2010, Hornbill, a provider of an ITIL® compatible service management platform, published the findings of a detailed survey, "ITIL®: State of the nation" that looked at international adoption and IT maturity. With over 500 respondents and 80%+ in executive and senior management roles, it painted a fair picture of the impact of ITIL® best practice on corporate IT.

Of those adopting ITIL®, 56% had chosen v2 and 44% were following v3. Of the 56% already with ITIL® v2, over 32% had elected to stick with this version, but many were introducing some of the v3 concepts. For those that had migrated to v3, it was simply the commonly adopted v2 processes (Incident, Problem and Change Management) that were upgraded. Practitioners embraced the familiar v2 processes still existed within the v3 Service Transition and Service Operation books and some of the new v3 processes that were already being managed by IT e.g. Security, Event Management and Request Fulfillment.

Although the Service Lifecycle approach was the top driver for upgrading to v3, it was evident that this had not been implemented or achieved. If the drive to adopt ITIL® v3 was coming from the top, CIOs would have lead with Service Strategy, but more often than not, it was IT operational staff pushing ITIL® up through the organization, so it is hardly surprising that an operational focus dominates.

The survey revealed that 68% had a medium to low level of ITSM maturity and these organizations faced common challenges to ITIL® adoption.

Insufficient Resources

Service improvement initiatives often stem from the desire to do *something* to break the cycle of firefighting that consumes IT resources. These organizations believe that ITIL® can increase efficiency, but are challenged to adopt a new way of working whilst maintaining business as usual.

Cultural Resistance

Technology focused IT staff may not be receptive to change and can find process overly bureaucratic. Creating a service culture requires a change in attitude and mindset and this is often the greatest challenge for adopters.

Business Sponsorship

ITIL® emphasizes the importance of securing backing from the business and whilst this is desirable, the business may not initially see the value and may view this as yet another IT 'project' that promises much, but delivers little.

Even the most ardent supporters would agree that ITIL is not perfect and although in theory "one size fits all", organizations really have to understand their current situation before planning the next step. One of the greatest mistakes made by adopters, is to embark on a project to 'implement ITIL®', without fully understanding the challenges they are trying to address, or setting measurable targets that enable them to identify when their goals have been achieved. ITIL® is not a means to an end; it is just one of the many tools that can be used to improve IT Service Management.

Ideally we would all start with Service Strategy, but if the IT organization is bleeding operationally, it will be far more difficult to adopt a strategic approach to service improvement. Technology-focused IT staff don't transform overnight into service-focused and business-aware employees because of ITIL® adoption. That requires evolution. By improving Attitude, Behavior and Culture, people have a better overall understanding of the aims and can ensure that processes are adopted to meet the chief objectives of improved service quality and customer satisfaction.

THE ITSM JOURNEY

It may help to look at ITSM as a journey that demands metamorphosis of the organization - a shift in focus and in culture - from managing IT within separate technology silos, to managing the end to end delivery of services using guidance from best practice frameworks. Those completely new to a best practice approach may be looking to adopt process, to bring order to a chaotic environment.

Organizations that approach ITIL® pragmatically, carefully plan their journey, and adopt the processes for which they are culturally ready, are the ones that see benefit. Know your starting point, where you are aiming to get to, how much effort you can afford to expend, along with how long you anticipate it will take to reach your goals. Along the way, you are likely to encounter obstacles that you didn't plan for, but if you don't take the time at the outset to consider and plan your progress, you are not very likely to reach your goals in a reasonable timeframe, if at all.

MAPPING THE JOURNEY

The ITIL® v2 publication, "Planning to implement service management" includes a model that depicts how IT organizations evolve. The diagram shows how influence on the business increases, as IT focus shifts from managing technology, through a number of growth stages, to IT as a value network, directly enabling business growth. The diagram below is adapted from the original publication.

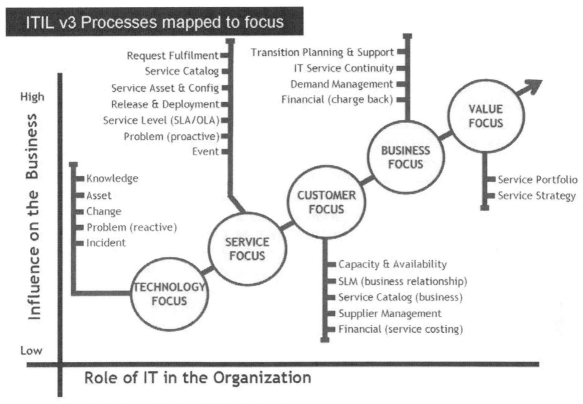

Figure 1

At each level in the model above, IT has a primary focus, a culture aligned to that focus and a corresponding level of process maturity. As the IT organization progresses through the phases of the ITSM journey, each shift in focus demands a shift in culture and the capacity to take new processes on board. The model suggests where processes fit within each area of focus, but there are no hard rules. Depending on the needs of your organization, it may be entirely reasonable to tackle more complex processes. However, if your IT organization has a technology focus, it will be incredibly difficult to adopt processes such as Service Portfolio, or Financial Management.

If your IT organization has a Technology Focus, the following characteristics should ring a few bells:

IT is split into separate technology silos with different groups having responsibility for servers, the network, databases etc. Although these separate technology domains serve the same business purpose e.g. enabling the Accounts team to issue invoices, or staff to communicate via email, IT doesn't always make the connection between the technology and the business outcome it serves.

Infrastructure and applications are largely treated as separate and unrelated domains. Improvements are centered on support processes rather than services. As a result, the business often views IT as purely a technology group, where costs need to be controlled. IT is the group that looks after the servers and tries to maintain a stable infrastructure so that other departments and employees can remain productive. The primary objective that the business sets for IT is to make the infrastructure more reliable, faster and cheaper than last year. Projects such as data enter consolidation, application consolidation and desktop standardization abound, as IT Management pursues its constant search for cost reduction and performance increases that can make IT run more efficiently.

STARTING WITH THE BASICS

Even the most chaotic IT organizations use some form of Incident, Problem and Change Management. Although the functions exist in day-to-day operation, it is unlikely that they are written down and usually exist inside the heads of IT heroes, who perform 'miracles' to keep the business operating and the users productive. IT is 100% focused on keeping the lights on and little or no time is available to focus on improvement. Incidents occur over and over again and changes are introduced into the infrastructure without considering the impact they may have on other IT systems.

The good news for IT organizations at the early stage of evolution is that adoption of just a few of the ITIL® processes can deliver real value. Taking a phased or bite-size approach and introducing processes that IT groups can identify with, reduces the risk of cultural resistance.

IT organizations seeking to break the circle of fire fighting adopt a small number of the ITIL® processes and seek to become proficient in these. The majority start with Incident, Problem, Change and basic Service Level Management.

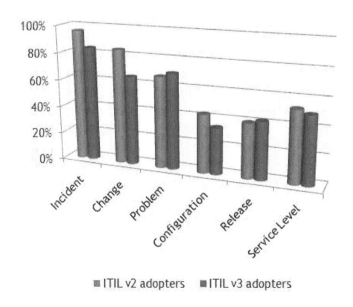

Figure 2 - *Source: Hornbill, ITIL®: State of the nation*

78

Incident Management

Although it may not be referred to using ITIL® terminology, every service/help desk will be running an Incident Management process. Building on this familiar process with a focus on improving the service experience drives customer satisfaction and improves perception of service quality.

Change Management

Industry research suggests that as many as 80% of Major Incidents are caused by inadequate Change Management. Not only can Change Management assist in reducing Incidents and stabilizing the infrastructure, it also reduces business risk and underpins IT governance.

Problem Management

Problem Management is one of the greatest aids in breaking the circle of fire-fighting. In the early stage of adoption, Problem Management is likely to be reactive, using trend analysis to suggest mechanisms that will reduce the number of incidents and improve service.

Service Level Management

Service Level Management (SLM) as described in the ITIL® books requires a level of business engagement that is not commonly found in technology focused IT operations. In the early stages of adoption, SLM is often restricted to IT setting its own targets for response and fix times, establishing a baseline for what can be achieved with existing resources.

Incident, Problem, Change, and Service Level Management enable IT to reduce fire-fighting, get the most from limited resources and stabilize the infrastructure. It is only by operating the processes that organisations gain the necessary levels of experience that enables them to mature. I would not advise anyone new to ITIL® to jump straight into the more complex processes, as they would probably find that they are biting off more than they can chew. Once IT has control of these basic processes, they typically seek to introduce further components from the framework to gain increased control of the technology and generate further efficiencies. Up to this point, momentum can be maintained with minimal impact on the IT culture, as the processes are familiar, easily understood, and are seen to work. Although IT effectiveness increases, it is at this stage of evolution that progress often stagnates, as continued investment in a focus on technology will deliver diminishing returns.

PEOPLE, PROCESS AND TECHNOLOGY

To successfully adopt any best practice framework, the organization must pay attention to people, process and technology, and it's no coincidence that the *people* component is listed first. Process is simply the flow of information and activities that are used to deliver the service; it's the creativity, innovation and attitude of the people using those processes that add real value to the customer experience.

Today we see a growing trend in the recruitment of service desk personnel, where customer service skills are considered more desirable than technical acumen. Service desks find it more effective to recruit customer service professionals and then teach them technical skills. The service desk is the customer's window to IT. By ensuring that it is manned by the right staff, with the right attitude and the right tools, IT can tackle service quality and customer satisfaction head on, instead of expecting processes alone to make a difference.

10 KEY CONSIDERATIONS WHEN ADOPTING ITSM

Service improvement is an on-going cycle and although there will be low hanging fruit, where small changes can deliver immediate results; this is no quick-fix. With the benefit of experience from successful ITSM initiatives and lessons learned from adoption, it's possible to provide some high-level advice to get your service improvement program started on the right track.

1. Successful ITSM initiatives are customer-centric

Far too many organizations approach best practice adoption from an IT perspective, prioritizing process and technology. People, communication and relationships should come first. Don't underestimate the effect of people and the impact that attitude, behavior and culture will have on success.

2. Be proactive

Don't wait for the customer to knock on your door and tell you what needs to be improved. Go and ask them and use their language, avoiding technical jargon. When defining your processes, consider running workshops and invite representatives from business units to ensure that you remain focused on improving the customer experience. Prioritize the improvements your customer's value most and determine the metrics they find useful. Keep checking, to make sure that things are moving in the right direction.

3. You need a vision and a plan

As the saying goes, a plan without a vision is like a sail without wind; it won't get you very far. Conduct an initial assessment. To make progress on your ITSM journey you will need to answer the following questions:

    a. Where do we want to be?
    b. Where are we now?
    c. What will it take to close the gaps?
    d. Where do we start?
    e. Who will be responsible for getting us there?
    f. How will we know when we've arrived?

Be mindful that your plan can be derailed by business as usual. To help avoid this, create a sense of urgency. Be realistic about what you can achieve within your timeframe, but if other things are seen as 'more important', progress will be slow and you face the risk of stagnation.

4. Get buy-in

Almost every presentation or conference session you attend on ITSM will advise the need for support from senior management. Don't try to sell ITIL®, the business won't be interested. Call your initiative

"Service Plus", "Business First", or anything else, but make sure it expresses the drive for improvement. If you can get business backing, it will certainly make things easier. However, management may initially be sceptical and you may have to prove that your efforts are making a difference before your service improvement initiative captures attention. Results speak for themselves, so know in advance what you can measure to prove your achievements and try wherever possible to link IT achievements to business measures e.g. goods being dispatched on time, or increased online bookings through improved service availability. If you initially struggle to get backing from senior management, don't despair. There are many examples of service delivery managers who have made great strides in service improvement without executive sponsorship, but with the support of engaged IT teams and people that were committed to making a difference.

5. Get help

If your budget allows, seek guidance from trusted professionals. There are many excellent firms, ranging from large organizations to independent consultants that can offer advice and help you to scope your deliverables. If your budget doesn't stretch this far, remember there are a number of organizations, such as HDI and itSMF, with hundreds, if not thousands of members, that can offer the benefit of their experiences. Attend conferences and get introduced to speakers and practitioners. People who bear the scars and wear the medals are generally happy to recount their experiences, or perhaps even invite you to visit and see their operation. Talk to the vendors; most will be willing to help, even if you are not in a position to purchase products or services. There is a wealth of experience available if you take the time to look for it.

6. Don't bite off more than you can chew

You don't need to boil the ocean; the basic Incident, Problem, Change and Service Level Management processes can make a huge difference to service quality. You may already be struggling with resource constraints, but you will need to dedicate time, people and budget to service improvement. Recognize that service may degrade whilst improvement measures are being implemented. Be mindful of tackling improvements that are outside your sphere of influence. If you have little influence on other areas of IT e.g. application development, you may wish to exclude this from your initial scope.

7. Weigh up the effort you can expend, against the value can expect

Countless IT organizations attempt relatively complex processes, such as building a Configuration Management System/Database (CMS/CMDB) without really asking the question, "What problem are we trying to solve?" Months, or even years of effort can be wasted on designing and implementing an overly complex solution, when perhaps a basic asset management register would have sufficed. Try to keep it simple.

8. Don't get sucked in by the latest 'fashionable' processes

There will always be hot topics and latest trends in ITSM. Service Catalog Management is currently on the agenda of many IT groups and there can be no doubt of the potential value, both for the customer and IT. However, if you don't already have robust Service Level Management and an understanding of service types, options and costs, you will struggle to deploy a service catalog. If there's a real need to enable users to request services, it may be more appropriate to offer a list of common service request types and allow users to initiate requests through a Self Service portal. Benefit can still be derived, but without the complexity of a full service catalog deployment.

9. Challenge demand on the Service Desk by eliminating 'dumb' contacts

The term 'dumb' does not fit well within a service lead approach. However, in this context, the term is not meant to be inflammatory. The phrase was coined in a book called "The best service is no service", where the authors advise about challenging the demand for service, instead of trying to cope with that demand. It expresses the concept that some services can be delivered without person-to-person interaction. Customers generally prefer to have access to some level of service without having to wait in line for someone to deal with their request. In the case of the IT service desk, contacts such as status enquiries, "Can you give me an update on...", or "I've forgotten my password", can easily be automated, diverted away from the service desk and placed in the hands of the customer. Removing those contacts creates the capacity the service desk needs to focus on resolution and more proactive activities.

10. Don't rest on your laurels

The Deming Cycle is often referenced in ITSM, with its stages of *Plan, Do, Check, Act*. Service improvement initiatives frequently fail to complete the cycle and it's said that too many ITSM programs suffer from *Plan, Do, Stop*. Once the initial goals and objectives have been reached, it's all too easy to think "We got there". By all means celebrate success, but remember, ITSM is about continual service improvement. When you have completed the first phase of your journey, it's time to revisit your plan and set the vision and priorities for the next phase.

SELECTING THE RIGHT TOOL

Purchasing or upgrading your service desk software is a strategic decision, which should only be made once you have identified your service and support needs. With roughly 200 vendors selling Service Desk and Service Desk tools and around 70 vendors playing in the mid-market and enterprise space, selecting the right tool is no easy task. Added to that is the complexity of selection if you are planning to implement a complete ITSM toolset. Whether you're looking at basic service desk ticketing, or more comprehensive service desk functionality, once you understand the scope, choosing the right tool and supplier helps establish the foundation you will need to deliver first class service.

UPGRADE, OR START FRESH

Before kicking off your selection process, be very clear about why you are looking for a new tool. IT organizations can be too quick to point the finger of blame at the current tool. In some cases the software may be more than capable, but perhaps needs to be upgraded to the latest version, or requires modification to address your requirements. Upgrading your current tool *can* be a less expensive and disruptive option.

On the flip side, organizations can make the mistake of assuming that upgrading will be cheaper and easier. Faced with losing business, the vendor may offer heavy discounts, or even free software, to tempt you to stick with the incumbent tool. *Beware of the cost of free.* Before you make the choice to stick with what you have, weigh up your relationship with the vendor. If they have not been supportive in the past, made promises they didn't keep, or suddenly paid less attention once they had your money – what will be different this time round? Don't make the mistake of going through an upgrade process, spending money on services and maintenance, only to realize shortly afterwards that you should have looked at alternative solutions. When making your decision to upgrade, or search for a new tool, by all means give your current supplier the opportunity, but if you've already lost confidence, perhaps it's time look to the market.

GET BUY-IN FROM MANAGEMENT

You may have settled on the need for a new tool, but don't waste time on the investigation process until you have some assurance that management are on side.

At the very least you'll need an elevator pitch, so that you can get approval to investigate. You'll need to be able to express; the greatest areas of pain, the challenges are you trying to solve and the impact of not solving those challenges. Every manager has issues that keep them aware at night, so be mindful of what's important to them. If your investigation process goes well and you identify your shortlist of tools, budget approval may be needed from outside of IT. Business managers will be less swayed by IT benefits, so you must be able to communicate the value your customers will derive from the new tool.

Remember, the business is mainly interested in two things: what will this cost and what can we expect in return?

Your service improvement program may be ambitious over the longer term, but try to avoid overstating your initial objectives. Be realistic about what you can achieve within reasonable timeframes. Successfully implementing a tool does not signal the end of your journey – it is the start. ITSM is about continual improvement and you will need management support and funding during subsequent phases. If you can show that you delivered the returns you initially stated, your chances of additional funding will have increased dramatically.

DO YOUR HOMEWORK

With so many vendors and a myriad of options, from basic ticketing systems to full ITSM suites, multiple deployment models and licensing options, the choice is staggering. Some tools are modular, enabling you to deploy what you need right now, adding extra modules as you need them, but appreciate the cost, time and effort required to add subsequent modules in the future. Other solutions offer an 'all you can eat' approach, with all modules bundled within the cost of the software. This model is attractive, but be careful not to try implementing too much too soon and appreciate that there may be other costs incurred, such as professional services, to get these modules into production.

Will Software as a Service (SaaS), or an on-premise model offer the best fit for your environment? SaaS can look appealing, as responsibility for maintaining the environment and carrying out upgrades falls to the vendor. In addition, upfront costs are typically lower than purchasing an on-premise solution. However, over the life of the software, SaaS is often the more expensive option. Industries, such as the financial and pharmaceuticals sectors may favor an on-premise solution to support regulatory compliance and demonstrate additional control and governance of the environment. Whatever your preferred deployment model, it pays to do your homework and understand the options that are available.

Licensing of software components can be complex, so be sure that you understand licensing options and can compare like-for-like. Fixed or named licenses are normally dedicated to specific users and are suitable for personnel that are permanently logged into the application e.g. the service desk. Concurrent, or floating licenses offer increased flexibility, allowing users to connect to the software when needed, but when they log out, licenses are made available to other users. Depending on the scope of your requirements you may need to consider other software components such as Self-Service, Asset Management or Knowledge base.

Depending on the scope of your initial requirements, components such as asset and event management, email capabilities, escalation/notification capabilities should be considered. Pay attention to functionality that can provide value to the customer. Self-service, knowledge base, and authorization features enable customers to help themselves, with the added benefit of reducing service desk workload.

RESOURCES FOR RESEARCH

There are numerous resources that you can draw upon to create your initial vendor list. Organizations use research from analyst groups, such as the Gartner, Forrester, or Ovum as a starting point. These groups are heavily engaged with the ITSM market and you may find it useful to speak with their analysts. Other resources, such as Pink Verify[1] (from Pink Elephant), lists vendors in terms of compatibility with ITIL® processes. If you're a member of industry groups, such as HDI, itSMF...seek advice from other members. Ask their opinion about tools you are considering to include in your selection process.

The explosion of social networks has tipped the balance of power to the consumer. Vendors can no longer hide behind marketing claims, as customers are more than willing to share their real-life product experiences. Linked-In® Groups are littered with comments and opinions from practitioners, which may help with your research, but be aware of the number of vendors and resellers monitoring these channels. Posting to one of these groups may solicit responses from people with a vested interest.

Other crowdsourcing lists can provide valuable insight without drawing attention from vendor sales staff. Chris Dancy of ServiceSphere has created a list[2] described as *"The 1st & most visible ITSM / ITIL® tools List, Crowdsourcing your FAVORITES."* The list is popular, as it enables people to vote for the tools they like or dislike, with practitioners adding comments about their experience with different tools. Although these resources are useful for research purposes and may prompt questions to ask the vendors, they offer no guarantee that any tool will be right for your environment.

FRAMEWORKS – ADOPT AND ADAPT

Many organizations dive straight into selecting a new service desk, leading with, "Must support the ITIL® framework." Although this is likely to be a major requirement, it should not be your primary consideration when selecting a tool. The global wave in adoption has driven vendors to produce ITIL® compatible' solutions and as a result, most commercial tools support the framework, but this offers no guarantee that the software will deliver what your organization needs. Conventional wisdom suggests that you need to have your processes defined before selecting a tool. Although there's certainly merit in following this advice, you may not have defined *all* your processes in advance. Even if you have, as your service improvement program evolves, your processes will need to adapt to reflect your increasing levels of maturity.

The majority of organizations adopting a best practice framework for the first time tend to focus on a small subset of processes; typically, Incident, Problem, Change and Service Level Management. In reality, you are probably using some, if not all of these processes already, but they may not be documented or formalized. Most tools are supplied with these basic processes out-of-the-box. Where possible, make use of these standard processes, but look for sufficient headroom and flexibility to enable you to change their behavior. Understand how the tool can be modified and the skills you will need if you intend to use internal resources for on-going configuration. Modern tools provide this flexibility and you should not need development resources to get the most from the software.

OUTLINING YOUR REQUIREMENTS

For any tool to produce results you need to be able to communicate the business need and explain the challenges you want to overcome. Organizations typically start their selection process with a document, or series of documents, that form a Request For Information (RFI).

---

[1] Pink Verify Certification - http://www.pinkelephant.com/pinkverify/
[2] ServiceSphere ITSM Tools List - http://list.ly/list/CD-itsm-tools

Because software is being purchased, RFI documents are often steered by technical staff and although the technical architecture is an important consideration, the technical bias should not outweigh the features of the solution that drive service quality and customer satisfaction. Involve customer service professionals with the specification of key requirements to maintain a focus on customer satisfaction, improved communication and the productivity of service desk staff.

REQUEST FOR INFORMATION

RFI documents are essential tools for assessing vendor suitability, so invest time up-front in their creation. Few vendors will want to engage in a sales cycle if they feel that their solution is not the right fit, so a well-constructed RFI will help all parties avoid wasting time and effort. Use the tools you already have available (spreadsheets, word processing etc) to create the RFI document(s). Although by no means exhaustive, Appendix B on Page 92 lists the main components that should be addressed when creating your RFI document(s):

ENGAGING WITH THE VENDORS

Once you've identified potential solutions and outlined your requirements, you should be ready to engage with the vendors. Send the RFI to 10-15 vendors that fit your initial selection criteria and provide a covering letter, asking the vendor to confirm their intent to respond.

Your initial list can reduce quite quickly, as some vendors may decide not to respond after digesting your requirements. You may also eliminate others based on the quality of their response and/or outline pricing. Use the scoring and weighting systems to evaluate the remaining responses and create your final shortlist. Ideally you will have three or four vendors remaining that can be taken forward to the next phase of the selection process.

THE DEMONSTRATION

The demonstration is an important part of the selection process, providing the opportunity for all stakeholders to meet the vendors and get an overview of the tools. Buy-in is essential, so ensure you have representation from parts of the organization that will be affected by the new tool.

To get the most from the demonstration, provide an agenda, allocating appropriate time slots for each area to be covered and ask vendors to stick to the format. To keep stakeholders engaged, structure your agenda so that your requirements are addressed up front, leaving vendor-related information until the end of the demonstration. You may find it beneficial to create real-life scenarios and ask vendors to demonstrate how the tools can meet your requirements in these areas. Allocated time slots can be quickly derailed by questions and answers during the demonstration, so decide how you will deal with this in advance. It may be better for stakeholders to take note of their questions and deal with these at the end of the demonstration.

It is advisable to create a scorecard that enables stakeholders to rate vendor demonstrations in accordance with a common set of criteria, but be aware that stakeholder impressions may change after seeing a series of vendors demonstrate their technologies. The vendor demonstration kit will contain example data and workflow that shows the tool in the best light, but these components may not be provided out of the box. Be very clear about what is included with a vanilla system and avoid making snap decisions, as your team will have to live with the tool for a long time. If time and resources allow, it will pay to carry out an evaluation of the tools that are top of your shortlist, based on stakeholder ratings.

THE EVALUATION AND PROOF OF CONCEPT

It can be all too easy to get drawn in by shiny new tools and flashy demonstrations that paint a picture of IT nirvana. Reality can be very different and using a tool in your own environment will provide a much deeper insight into how the tool can work for you. Vendors are typically open to providing on-site evaluations, or even participating in a deeper proof of concept deployment.

An evaluation is typically carried out using your own resources and a small amount of support from the vendor. The tool is deployed with a vanilla configuration and the vendor may provide an overview of the technology and access to their support team, so that your team are prepared for the evaluation. There are a number of distinct benefits to this approach. Your team will appreciate what is provided out of the box, determine ease of use and understand whether your own resources can manage the tool on an on-going basis. If your shortlist has been whittled down to two or three tools, evaluation should provide you with a level of deeper understanding and help you to choose a preferred vendor. If the vendor is prepared to offer an evaluation, ensure that you dedicate sufficient resources to complete the process in a timely manner and use mandatory requirements from your RFI as an evaluation checklist.

If your requirements demand more in-depth customization the tool, integration with other technologies or exposing the tool to your end users, your evaluation team will not have the requisite skills and you will probably need help. The vendor can usually provide resources to install, configure, and integrate the tool, but it is reasonable for the vendor to charge for these services. However, a paid proof of concept need not cost the earth, or have a material impact on the project's budget. Once you have identified your preferred supplier, it should be possible to isolate one or two processes and ask the vendor to implement the tool with this limited scope. Using the tool to sense check your process, with your data, in your environment should provide genuine insight into its capabilities. This mitigates risk, as your financial exposure is limited to the services provided and not the cost of entire software and maintenance package. If you decide to proceed, any requirements already delivered during the proof of concept should be reusable in your production system.

NEGOTIATION

When making any purchase, particularly of high cost items, we like to feel that we've negotiated the best possible deal and secured maximum value from our available budget. Although vendors are normally prepared to be flexible, be realistic about the level of discount you expect them to concede. Eating into vendor profits may mean that the deal becomes unpalatable and corners may be cut to reduce costs. Pay particular attention to professional services and project management costs. Cutting too deeply in these areas may result in a partly delivered solution that doesn't meet your requirements.

Some vendors may be prepared to offer a money back guarantee on software and maintenance components in the event that the solution does not meet your stated requirements. If such a guarantee is offered, it will normally have certain restrictions and you should expect to pay for services that the vendor has already delivered. However, a guarantee will go a long way towards mitigating your risk and ensures that you are not committed to a tool that falls short of meeting your needs.

Look for win-win opportunities during negotiation e.g. the vendor may be looking to secure case studies, or reference sites. Provided your corporate marketing does not restrict such activities, you made be able to secure concessions by offering to speak with prospective customers, or at industry events, with the caveat that you are happy with the solution.

Whilst in no way definitive, the steps outlined above will mitigate your risks and help you avoid common mistakes. Do your homework, understand your options, address each step and you will select an ITSM tool that is fit for purpose and fully utilized by staff.

NOTES

A BEGINNING, NOT AN END

There you have it. In less than 100 pages we've tried our best to give you the hard and soft sides of managing a successful Service Desk. It goes without saying that there is much more to this wonderful and satisfying career than we could cover in even 500 more pages. And that brings us to the final and, perhaps, most sturdy piece of advice in the *Service Desk Manager's Crash Course*: *There's no substitute for testing what you know or for the wisdom that your experience will bring.*

You're done crashing; time to get cracking....

APPENDIX A

SAMPLE EFFECTIVE INTERVIEW QUESTIONS

1. What is motivating your decision to leave your current job?

2. Describe in detail what ideally you would be doing in your next position. What type of company would you work with, who would you report to, what types of projects would you be working on?

3. On a scale of 1 to 5, 1 being very happy where you are and 5 being ready to start a new job in two weeks, how would you rate your motivation level to make a change?

4. How do you ensure quality work and communication to customers?

5. How are urgent situations handled?

6. How would co-workers and customers describe your decision making style?

7. Name an exceptional experience you gained from a recent customer support issue and how will it affect your next call?

8. Who is ultimately responsible for quality?

9. How would you describe yourself?

10. How do you determine or evaluate success? Give me an example of one of your successful accomplishments.

11. Do you have the qualifications and personal characteristics necessary for success in your chosen career?

12. What has been your most rewarding accomplishment?

13. What motivates you to put forth your greatest effort?

14. Can you describe your long-range goals and objectives?

15. Before you can make a productive contribution to the company, what degree of training do you feel you will require?

16. Tell me what you know about our company.

17. Why did you decide to seek a position in this company?

18. What level of compensation would it take to make you happy?

19. Give me a specific occasion in which you conformed to a policy with which you did not agree.

20. Tell me about a time when you had to go above and beyond the call of duty in order to get a job done.

21. Recall a time from your work experience when your manager or supervisor was unavailable and a problem arose. What was the nature of the problem? How did you handle that situation? How did that make you feel?

22. How do you determine priorities in scheduling your time? Give examples.

23. Tell of a time when your active listening skills really paid off for you - maybe a time when other people missed the key idea being expressed.

24. Tell of the most difficult customer service experience that you have ever had to handle -- perhaps an angry or irate customer. Be specific and tell what you did and what was the outcome.

25. Give an example of when you had to work with someone who was difficult to get along with. Why was this person difficult? How did you handle that person?

26. What is the biggest mistake you've made?

27. Tell me about a time when you came up with an innovative solution to a challenge your company/class/organization was facing. What was the challenge? What role did others play?

28. Tell me about a time when you failed to meet a deadline. What things did you fail to do? What were the repercussions? What did you learn?

29. Describe a time when you put your needs aside to help a co-worker or classmate understand a task. How did you assist him or her? What was the result?

APPENDIX B

HOW TO COMPOSE A REQUEST FOR INFORMATION

Requirements Specification and RFI Process

This document sets the scene, enabling vendors to understand your current situation, greatest challenges and areas of pain. It explains your high level requirements and desired outcomes, but avoids functional detail. As a minimum, provide an outline of the following:

- Description of the Business
- Environment and services supported
- Overview of the IT function and current ITSM tools
- Major challenges and areas of pain
- Statement of requirements and desired outcomes (high level)
- Format of the RFI (listing documents included)
- Instructions for vendor acknowledgement of receipt/intent to respond
- Instructions for vendors on how to format their response
- Timescales for key stages of the RFI process
- Anticipated implementation plan/phases
- Explanation of evaluation and scoring of vendor responses
- Process for RFI clarification and submitting questions
- Contractual terms and conditions

Technical Specification

The tool should operate effectively alongside your current technical architecture and enable you to take advantage of skills you already have in-house e.g. database administration, or integration with existing tools such as asset and event management. Outline your current technical architecture and request assurance of the technical fit by asking the vendor to provide:

- Architectural overview of solution
- Databases supported
- Browsers supported
- Email systems supported
- Server / Client hardware and Operating System specifications
- Operation on virtualized/thin client platforms
- Failover and backup requirements
- Archival and storage requirements
- Network specifications (speed, bandwidth, protocols)
- Security and authentication
- Integration with existing tools
- Scalability options for future growth

Functional Specification

Modern ITSM tools provide an impressive level of functionality and with the technology constantly evolving, even the mid-market tools now include more functionality than most IT departments are capable of deploying. Therefore it is important to differentiate between functional requirements that are:

- *Mandatory – will be used from go-live date*
- *Highly Desirable - expect to use in the near future*
- *Desirable - expect to use in the medium to longer term.*

Using ranking system such as this enables vendor responses to be scored, with higher points awarded for meeting mandatory requirements.

Although vendors may be able to claim compliance with functional requirements, it is important you appreciate what is available out of the box, versus what needs to be customized. Backed with clear instructions to vendors, a simple scoring system will offer increased visibility of the effort required to deliver against each functional requirement.

- *0 – Requirement cannot be met*
- *1 – Requirement partially met through customization*
- *2 – Requirement partially met out of the box*
- *3 – Requirement fully met through customization*
- *4 – Requirement fully met out of the box*

Using these ranking and scoring systems creates a more level playing field, making it easier for you to rate vendor responses.

You will also need to consider your existing data. If it's in reasonable shape, you may wish to port current user/customer, asset and knowledge data into the new tool. However, don't be tempted to recreate a mirror image of your existing system. Implementing a new tool is an ideal time for you to question the value of the data you already hold and offers a great opportunity to review how your data should be structured. For example; does your current incident categorization support your ability to make decisions about the areas you need to focus on?

Many organizations are satisfied with the vendor's claim that they provide hundreds of canned reports, but in reality, the majority will not provide what you need out-of-the-box. Ensure that you have scoped the creation of critical reports into your implementation plan and that you understand the skills you will need to create and modify your own reports without having to rely on specialist skills.

Pricing Schedule

Organizations typically look at initial, or year one costs, but often fail to consider on-going charges when selecting a new tool. Ideally your RFI will include a pricing template that enables you to compare vendor proposals. The pricing template should require vendors to provide a projection of total cost of ownership over the anticipated life of the software, typically 5 years. The template should make provision for the following costs:

- Software licenses for mandatory components
- Software licenses for desirable components
- Software licenses for test/backup/development purposes
- Software maintenance and support for mandatory components (years 1 -5)
- Software maintenance and support for desirable components (years 1 -5)
- Professional services to deliver against stated requirements
- Breakdown of Professional services costs (implementation, customization, integration, consulting, project management)
- Education and training
- Expenses
- Day rates for additional/on-going vendor services (consulting, development, etc.)
- Total cost (Year 1)
- Estimated total cost of ownership (Years 1-5)

Project and Implementation Approach

Even if the tool can meet all of your needs, a properly scoped and well executed implementation plan is essential to ensure success. It can be tempting to use your own resources in an effort to reduce the cost of purchase, but this can be false economy. Your personnel will not have the depth of experience, or the best practice approach that the vendor can call upon, so ensure that your RFI includes a section that outlines relevant components of the vendor implementation plan.

- Implementation approach and methodology
- Project plan and documentation
- Acceptance testing process
- Outline of infrastructure preparation effort
- Outline of vendor/own resources required
- Skills required to implement and support the tool
- Knowledge transfer process
- Outline of training courses

Support and Maintenance

Successful on-going operation relies upon dependable support and maintenance services from the tool vendor. To protect your investment you will also need the option to upgrade the software when new releases are made available. Ensure your RFI outlines your support and maintenance requirements and request confirmation of:

- Standard support offering
- Support offering for extended hours (if applicable)
- Details of any warranties provided
- Service Level Agreement details (target response, resolution times)

- Current release version of application
- Percentage of customers on current release version
- Process for capturing enhancement requests
- Application roadmap and release plan for future versions
- Quality assurance and testing process
- Outline of upgrade process for major and minor releases
- Effort and cost to upgrade
- Escrow arrangements

Vendor Profile and References

Establishing a partnership with the right vendor is crucial to successful implementation and on-going operation of the tool. Ask questions about the vendor organization, background and financial viability to support due diligence, but don't forget to look for evidence of reputation, integrity and service differentiators. Ensure you request information about their customers and vendor involvement in both their user, and the wider ITSM community.

- Company name, address and contact information
- Company structure, number of employees dedicated to products and services proposed
- History of supplying the products and services proposed
- Applicable quality standards, certification and awards
- Industry vision and medium to long term business objectives
- Participation and influence within the ITSM industry
- Statement of understanding (how your requirements will be met)
- Differentiators (how the vendor can offer additional value)
- General comments (any additional information that may assist evaluation)
- Evidence of user group
- Examples of similar customer implementations
- Customer references (3-5 to be taken up only if shortlisted)

Bear in mind that vendors are unlikely to offer references with customers that have had a poor experience, so search for evidence within the customer, or wider ITSM community to validate the experience of other customers.

REFERENCES, IDEAS, AND SUGGESTIONS

Team Building

- Dinner Out
    - o Restaurants
    - o Grill at someone's house
- Bring families together for dinner
    - o Picnic at the park
    - o Bring Dinner In
    - o Grill on site outside the office (Parking lot)
    - o Catered BBQ
    - o Sandwiches
    - o Pizza
    - o Chinese Food
- Fantasy Sports – Just make sure they don't spend too much time at work shuffling their team around.
    - o Football
    - o Baseball
    - o Hockey
    - o Basketball
- Bowling
- Horseback Riding
- Cruise to Nowhere
- Whitewater Rafting
- Go Karts
- Mini Golf
- Gaming Center
- Batting Cages
- Day on the Lake
- Movie
    - o In House (Projectors work nicely)
    - o To the theater
- Paintball
- Golfing - Rent Carts for added excitement
- Scavenger Hunt
- Rock Climbing Wall
- Sports Outings
    - o Major or Minor League Baseball
    - o Major or Minor League Hockey
    - o Basketball
    - o Football
    - o Soccer
    - o College Sports

- Philanthropy
  - Adopt a Highway
  - Charity Run/Walk
  - Dog Walks
  - Bicycling Events
- Theme Parks
- Halloween Party
- Trip to the Beach
- Team Retreat
  - Mountains
  - Beach
  - Camping
- Play Volleyball
- Kickball
- Play Kickball
- Play Softball
- Join a Softball League
- See a Play
- See a Musical
- Ropes Courses
- Adventure Trails
- www.RecipeforSuccess.com
- www.**Team**Builders.com/Programs
- www.audience-response-solutions.com
- www.afterburnerseminars.com
- www.StrategicAdventures.com
- www.hikebikekayak.com
- www.adventureassoc.com
- **www.team**bonding.com

Other Sources for Ideas: BOOKS

- **Quick Teambuilding Activities for Busy Managers: 50 Exercises That Get Results in Just 15 Minutes** by Brian Cole Miller
- **More Quick Team-Building Activities for Busy Managers: 50 New Exercises That Get Results in Just 15 Minutes** by Brian Cole Miller
- **The Big Book of Team Building Games: Trust-Building Activities, Team Spirit Exercises, and Other Fun Things to Do** by John W. Newstrom and Edward E. Scannell
- **Team-Building Activities for Every Group** by Alanna Jones
- **Team Challenges: 170+ Group Activities to Build Cooperation, Communication, and Creativity** by Kris Bordessa
- **The Big Book of Humorous Training Games** by Doni Tamblyn and Sharyn Weiss
- **Indoor/Outdoor Team Building Games For Trainers: Powerful Activities From the World of Adventure-Based Team Building and Ropes Courses** by Harrison Snow
- **The Big Book of Customer Service Training Games** by Peggy Carlaw and Vasudha Kathleen Deming
- **The Big Book of Customer Service Training Games (Big Book)** by Peggy Carlaw and Vasudha K. Deming

DETAILED IT SKILLS MATRIX EXAMPLE

Legend
0 = No skill
1 – Beginning
2 – Intermediate
3 – Expert

TECHNICAL

	SQL Server 2005 Admin	Outlook	Windows XP	Windows 2003 Server	Exchange Server 2000
Associate	3	3	3	3	2
Associate	1	2	2	1	1
Associate	0	2	2	1	0
Associate	0	2	3	3	1
Associate	0	2	3	2	2

Skill Level Average (Target 2.3)	0.8	2.2	2.6	2	1.2

PROFESSIONAL/SOFT SKILLS

	Time Management	Critical Thinking	Initiative	Phone	Technical Writing
Associate	3	3	1	3	0
Associate	2	0	2	2	1
Associate	2	0	0	0	1
Associate	3	1	2	2	3
Associate	3	1	2	2	0

Skill Level (Target 2.3)	2.6	1	1.4	1.8	1

CERTIFICATIONS

	CompTIA Network +	MCP	MCSE	ITIL Foundations Certification	HDI Support Center Analyst (SCA)
Associate	X	X	X	X	X
Associate	X	X	X		X
Associate			X	X	X
Associate				X	
Associate	X		X	X	

MORE REFERENCES, IDEAS AND SUGGESTIONS

We hope *Service Desk Manager's Crash Course* has gotten you started on your way to being a successful Service Desk Manager. We tried to put enough of everything in the book so you could get off the ground as a new manager and get started with something useful TODAY, and have a handy reference guide for those times when you are stuck and don't know where else to go.

Join the conversation with almost 1000 of your peers in our private LinkedIn group:
http://www.linkedin.com/groups?home=&gid=1948610

If you have any questions about anything discussed in the book, please send an e-mail to authors@servicedeskcrashcourse.com and Phil will try to respond to you via e-mail, or by addressing it in a feature article on the website.

Thanks for reading!

Phil Gerbyshak

ABOUT THE AUTHOR:

Phil Gerbyshak

Phil Gerbyshak is the chief connections officer who works with small businesses and organizations to increase employee & customer engagement by using social media to create and build relationships. He helps them understand it's really not about the tools; it's all about the conversations they participate in and the connections they create and cultivate.

Phil worked in IT for the past 15 years, and has focused his efforts on understanding and leveraging the social media space for over 5 years. His work building relationships using blogs was spotlighted in the 2005 book What Nobody Ever Tells You About Blogging and Podcasting: Real Life Advice from 101 People Who Successfully Leverage the Power of the Blogosphere.

In addition to doing keynote and breakout addresses, Phil greatly enjoys coaching others in the simple strategies and tactics that make life great. His first book 10 Ways to Make It Great! was published in 2006 and inspired many to make the changes in their life to go from good...to GREAT.

His second book Help Desk Manager's Crash Course offers managers a guidebook for hiring, firing, discipline, and more.

His latest book #Twitterworks features success stories, tips and traps about using twitter for independent restaurants and small businesses.

Phil is currently working on several projects to enable small businesses to effectively use social media in a concentrated amount of time.

In a nutshell, Phil does speaking, coaching, and training for small and medium sized organizations and entrepreneurs who want to take their life, and their business to the next level.

Recession Proof Your Life: Make a PLAN and Make It Great!

Driven to bring results to your business, Phil has developed an enlightening and stimulating PLAN for business people and entrepreneurs looking to watch their dreams take off. This distinctive method of pushing beyond your barriers has helped countless people live their lives with passion and focus. Phil has a charming and delightful personality, which brings warmth and personal interaction with his audience. When Phil speaks with your organization, you will feel as though he was chatting with you one-on-one. Phil's action PLAN includes...

- **Purpose –** Define your dreams and go after them whole-heartedly. Phil gives you the tools to hone in on the life you have always wanted, but were too afraid to go after.

- **Learning –** Once you have established your purpose in life, you can then find out all of the necessary information to go after it! Phil encourages you to expand your mind and your network, as you seek out the right path for your life.

- **Attitude –** Your attitude will determine the amount of your success, and the quality of your life. Phil explains how a winning attitude will always come out on top.

- **Network –** Along the adventure of life, you will meet many people along the way. Phil teaches you how to engage these people, and build quality relationships that will bring you closer to your dreams faster than you ever imagined.

With a PLAN to *Make It Great!*, life's challenges will be far easier to navigate. Phil has spent his life dedicated to helping others succeed, and offers his timeless wisdom in speaking engagements across the world. His winning smile and bubbling exuberance has earned him the title of Relationship Geek, and he encourages each of you to Make a PLAN and *Make It Great!*

Phil Gerbyshak: Powerful Professional Speaker

Phil gives of his time and energy to every person he meets. Vibrant, with a radiant smile and sparkling personality, Phil has given thousands of people the keys to engaging business relationships. His speeches have touched the lives of people from around the world, who were looking for a better way to live their dreams. Phil has the solution, and is devoted to sharing his knowledge with all who would love to hear it.

The incredible benefits of Phil's presentations are too valuable to be missed. His ability to be personable, enlightening, and practical is a combination guaranteed to bring success and energy to any business or organization. Your business will thrive on the relationship building strategies that Phil passionately shares at each of his speaking engagements.

Phil has lived a heartwarming and inspirational life, zealously pursuing his dreams. Each day, Phil does what it takes to *Make It Great!* Learn more about the proactive steps to success that Phil can teach your business by contacting Phil today.

Contact Phil today to have him Make your organization GREAT!

Phone:	414-640-7445
Email:	phil@philgerbyshak.com
Blog:	http://makeitgreatguy.com
Website:	http://philgerbyshak.com

SERVICE DESK MANAGER'S CRASH COURSE

HOW TO HIRE THE BEST AND AVOID THE REST

KEYS TO BUILDING STRONG TEAMS — AND KEEPING THEM

TIPS FOR MAKING APPRAISALS MORE POWERFUL TOOLS

THE DO'S AND DON'TS OF DELEGATION

METRICS FOR MORE FOCUSED GOAL-SETTING

SIMPLE STEPS TO GET ONE DESK UP AND RUNNING — OR TEN

IT SERVICE MANAGEMENT 101

THE INS AND OUTS OF ITIL®

SERVICE DESK MANAGER'S CRASH COURSE

PHIL GERBYSHAK

This page left intentionally blank

ISBN: 978-1469935737

For ordering bulk quantities, please contact Phil Gerbyshak at phil@philgerbyshak.com.

For ordering individual books, please go to Amazon and search for Service Desk Manager's Crash Course or insert ISBN: 978-1469935737

SERVICE DESK MANAGER'S CRASH COURSE

Made in the USA
Lexington, KY
14 November 2012